# MICHEL FABER

WRITERS AND THEIR WORK

SERIES EDITORS:

*Professor Dinah Birch CBE,
University of Liverpool
Professor Dame Janet Beer,
University of Liverpool*

*Writers and Their Work*, launched in 1994 in association with the British Council, won immediate acclaim for its publication of brief but rigorous critical examinations of the works of distinguished writers and schools of writing. The series embraces the best of modern literary theory and criticism, and features studies of many popular contemporary writers, as well as the canonical figures of literature and important literary genres.

© Copyright 2023 by Rodge Glass

First published in 2023 by
Liverpool University Press
4 Cambridge Street
Liverpool L69 7ZU

on behalf of
Northcote House Publishers Ltd
Mary Tavy
Devon PL19 9PY

Rodge Glass has asserted the right to be identified as the author of this book in accordance with the Copyright, Designs and Patents Act 1988. All rights reserved. No part of this book may be reproduced, stored in a retrieval system, or transmitted, in any form or by any means, electronic, mechanical, photocopying, recording, or otherwise, without the prior written permission of the publisher.

**British Library Cataloguing-in-Publication Data**
A catalogue record for this book is available from the British Library

ISBN 978-1-83764-477-3

Typeset by Carnegie Book Production, Lancaster
Printed and bound by CPI Group (UK) Ltd, Croydon CR0 4YY

# MICHEL FABER

## Rodge Glass

NORTHCOTE

'One of the most absurd tragedies about us as a species is that each of us is convinced we're misunderstood, alone, a misfit. There doesn't seem to be anybody in the world who feels they're what a standard-issue human being ought to be. Literature reminds us of this paradox – our specialness and our commonality.'

Michel Faber

For Lucia and Cora, always

# Contents

| | |
|---|---:|
| *Acknowledgements* | ix |
| *Biographical Outline* | xi |
| *Abbreviations* | xv |
| Introduction | 1 |
| 1. Faber's World of the Short Story | 7 |
| 2. Faber's World of the Novella (or Medium-Sized Story) | 31 |
| 3. Faber's World of the Novel | 53 |
| 4. Faber's World of *The Crimson Petal* | 81 |
| 5. Faber's World of Verse | 105 |
| 6. Faber, Out of Time: A Look Back, A Look Forward | 113 |
| *Notes* | 119 |
| *Select Bibliography* | 125 |
| *Index* | 129 |

Unpublished illustration by Michel Faber, Henry Rackham and Emmeline Fox from *The Crimson Petal and the White*

# Acknowledgements

A book of literary criticism is a joint effort.

This volume represents my independent take on Michel Faber's works, but I have welcomed correspondence with my subject. Thanks to Michel for giving generously of his time and energy to correspond with me, over several years. Thanks to my editor Christabel Scaife, to the University of Dundee's Archive Services, who allowed access to their Canongate archive, to Judy Moir, Faber's long-time editor, and to Francis Bickmore, Publisher at Large at Canongate Books. Thanks to Alex Marsden, Academic Production Editor at Carnegie Book Production, and especially to copy editor Claire Taylor-Jay for her attentive and careful work.

And thank you, for reading.

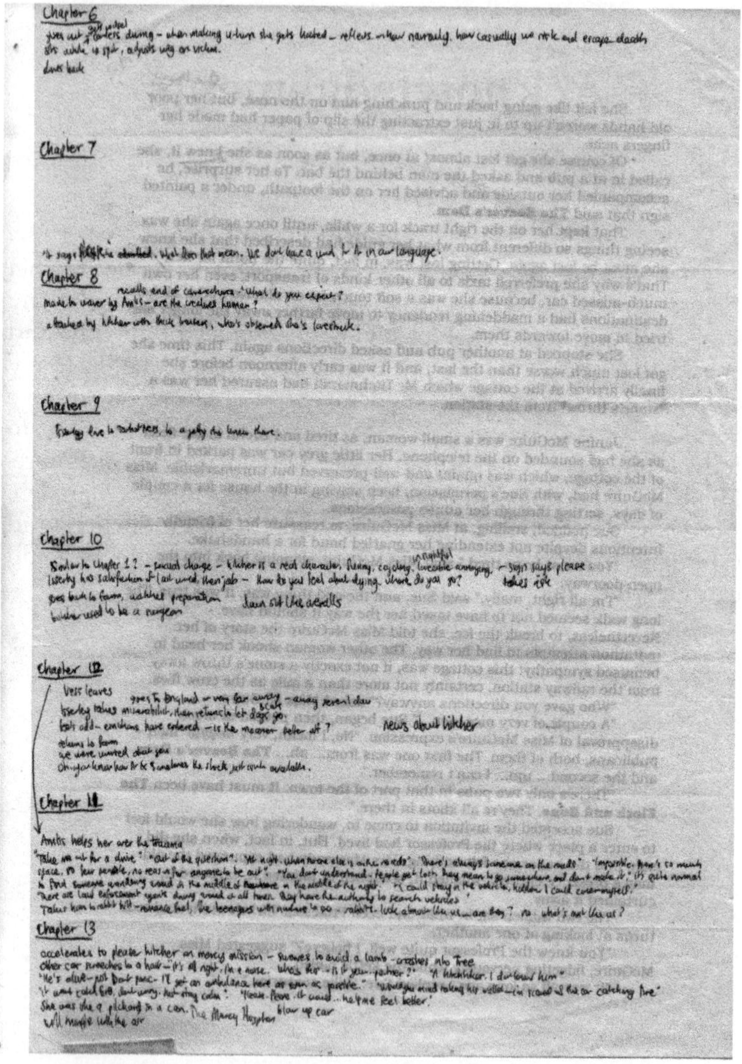

Handwritten schema for *Under the Skin*, by Michel Faber

# Biographical Outline

| | |
|---|---|
| 1960 | Born 13th April in The Hague, the Netherlands. |
| 1967 | Moves with parents to Melbourne, Australia. An older half-brother and half-sister remain in the Netherlands. |
| 1968 | First attempt at fiction, illustrated primary-school pamphlet 'Knabbel and Babbel Go to the Moon'. |
| 1971–1975 | Attends Boronia High then Bayswater High schools. Drafts many short stories, abandoning most, burning some. Starts attempting novels. |
| 1976 | Starts to conceive of a non-fiction book about music he would like to write. Over the next 40-plus years, his sense of what it might contain keeps changing. |
| 1979 | Drafts first 100 pages of *The Crimson Petal and the White*. Marries first wife Grayson Gerrard, in secret, during third year at University of Melbourne. |
| 1980 | Graduates with a 2:1 in English Language and Literature (modules include Dutch Literature, Philosophy and Rhetoric). Might have gained a 1st, but accidentally walks out of one exam early, mistakenly thinking he had finished. |
| 1984 | Writes first two poems, 'Old Age, in Our Sleep' and 'Old People in Hospital'. Versions of both will appear in *Undying* 32 years later. First version of 'Fish' drafted. |
| 1987 | Aged 27, completes draft of *The Crimson Petal*. Writes novel *A Photograph of Jesus*. |
| 1988 | Meets Eva Youren in Melbourne, a woman of Polish-German heritage from a family of Jehovah's Witnesses. |

| | |
|---|---|
| 1993 | Moves to Scottish Highlands, 40 miles north of Inverness, with Eva, her two sons Ben and Daniel, also Eva's previous husband, David. David lives in Tain, while Faber and Eva live on Tarrel Farm near Portmahomack, eight miles away. The children move between households. Michel works in a care home until Eva suggests he concentrate on his writing. |
| 1996 | Wins St James Short Story Award for 'Some Rain Must Fall', also Macallan Short Story Award for 'Fish'. 'Fish' broadcast on BBC Radio Scotland. |
| 1997 | Wins Neil M. Gunn Award for 'Half a Million Pounds and a Miracle'. Offered contract with Canongate for collection of stories, Faber accepts. Serious work on then-titled *Underneath the Skin* begins. |
| 1998 | First book, *Some Rain Must Fall* (short stories), published. November: Faber's editor Judy Moir recommends Canongate publish Faber's debut novel. |
| 1999 | Editorial completed on *Under the Skin*. Writes third poem, 'Old Bird, Not Very Well'. Story 'Taking Care of Big Brother', which the author had thought rejected by the BBC, produced by David Jackson Young, broadcast on BBC Radio 4. *Some Rain Must Fall* wins Saltire Society First Book of the Year Award. Moves to Fearn Station House. |
| 2000 | Second book, *Under the Skin* (novel), published. Sells to 20 publishers worldwide. Shortlisted for Whitbread First Novel Award, nominated for Dublin International IMPAC Award. Embarks on re-writing and research for *The Crimson Petal*. |
| 2001 | Third book, *The Hundred and Ninety-Nine Steps* (novella), published. |
| 2002 | Fourth book, *The Courage Consort* (novella), published in February. Fifth published book, *The Crimson Petal and the White* (novel), in October, becomes international bestseller. *Under the Skin* nominated for Dublin IMPAC Award. In December, writes *Crimson Petal* story 'Christmas in Silver Street'. |

BIOGRAPHICAL OUTLINE

| | |
|---|---|
| 2005 | In January, writes *Crimson Petal* story 'Chocolate Hearts from the New World', issued as limited edition chapbook in US. Sixth book, *The Fahrenheit Twins* (short stories), published. Features 'The Safehouse', runner-up in first National Short Story Prize. Marries Eva Youren. |
| 2006 | Seventh book, *The Apple: Crimson Petal Stories*, published. |
| 2006 | Short story 'Bye Bye Natalia' published in *Granta 94*. Nonfiction essay 'Dreams in the Dumpster, Language Down the Drain' published in *Not One More Death* (Verso Books), responding to wars in Iraq and Afghanistan. Withdraws from public life. |
| 2007 | US edition of *The Fahrenheit Twins*, minus titular story, re-titled *Vanilla Bright like Eminem*, published. Song 'Steam Comes off Our House' by Scottish band De Rosa, with lyrics by Faber, appears on Chemikal Underground compilation *Ballads of the Book*. |
| 2008 | Eighth book, *The Fire Gospel* (novel), published as part of Canongate Myths series. Eva diagnosed with cancer. |
| 2009 | 'Walking After Midnight' appears in *Ox-Tales: Water*, published by Oxfam, an excerpt from forthcoming *The Book of Strange New Things*. |
| 2010 | Faber contributes story 'A Flash of Blue Light' to *Elsewhere*, a four-book collaboration between Glasgow-based indie publisher Cargo, McSweeney's in US and Edinburgh Book Festival. |
| 2011 | Acclaimed BBC TV adaptation of *The Crimson Petal and the White*, starring Romola Garai, Chris O'Dowd and Gillian Anderson, aired, sold across Europe. Makes limited return to public life, to travel with Eva while she is able. |
| 2013 | Jonathan Glazer-directed film adaptation of *Under the Skin* released, starring Scarlett Johannson. Experimental score written by Mica Levi. Nominated for, wins numerous international awards. Faber and Eva attend screening at BFI, London when Eva is seriously ill. She leaves hospital for one evening to see the film. |

| | |
|---|---|
| 2014 | Faber lives in Room 212 of Parkside Hospital, London, for several months while Eva is a patient there. She dies on Sunday 6th July. Ninth book, *The Book of Strange New Things* (novel), published. Faber says Eva told him to change the ending to have 'less cleverness and more emotional resonance', urging him to finish it. |
| 2015 | *The Book of Strange New Things* wins Saltire Society Scottish Book of the Year. Ten-episode BBC Radio 4 adaptation airs in October 2014. 2016: Tenth book, *Undying: A Love Story* (poetry), published. Includes Foreword providing context, detailing history of poems included. *The Book of Strange New Things* nominated for Dublin IMPAC Award. |
| 2017 | Pilot of *Oasis*, TV series based on *The Book of Strange New Things*, aired on Amazon Prime. |
| 2020 | Eleventh book, *D: A Tale of Two Worlds* (novel for children), published by Transworld. First critical volume on the author's work, *Michel Faber: Critical Essays*, published. Faber writes Foreword. |
| 2020–2022 | Works on *Listen*, due to be published by Canongate in Autumn 2023. This is the culmination of the idea he first had for a non-fiction book about music. |

# Abbreviations

**CRITICAL WORK**

MFCE   Rebecca Langworthy, Kristin Lindfield-Ott and Jim MacPherson (eds.), *Michel Faber: Critical Essays*

**FABER WORKS**

| | |
|---|---|
| BSNT | *The Book of Strange New Things* |
| D | *D: A Tale of Two Worlds* |
| HNNS | *The Hundred and Ninety-Ninety Steps* |
| POJ | *A Photograph of Jesus* |
| SRMF | *Some Rain Must Fall* |
| TA | *The Apple: Crimson Petal Stories* |
| TCC | *The Courage Consort* |
| TCP | *The Crimson Petal and the White* |
| TFG | *The Fire Gospel* |
| TFT | *The Fahrenheit Twins* |
| ULS | *Undying: A Love Story* |
| UTS | *Under the Skin* |

# Introduction

How best to introduce the work of a writer like Michel Faber, whose work over the last 25 years so resists categorization? Who, for decades before that, did not seek out publication at all, and whose every new creation aims to be meaningfully different from his others? That is the challenge of this book, which interrogates Faber's unusually diverse work across genre and form. His various books feature elements readers may recognize from science fiction, horror, thriller, historical fiction, romance and other genres – but these often overlap, influencing and complicating each other. Form, chronology and genre are all problematized by Faber's approach to hybridization, his habit of subverting reader expectations, also crucially the nature of his creative process, which often sees multiple projects in process for long periods. Early sections of *The Crimson Petal and the White* were written as a teenage undergraduate, though it became his fifth published book. The unpublished *A Photograph of Jesus* influenced the later and lauded *The Book of Strange New Things*, while his latest novel, *D*, is rooted in unpublished work started 30 years ago. This is not a writer whose projects can be easily divided into clear, chronological chunks. Neither does Faber fit easily into any one identifiable national or cultural tradition. Born in the Netherlands, raised in Australia, then embraced in Scotland by writers and readers alike before moving to England after his wife's death, perceptions of Faber are sometimes influenced by the author's transnationalism, and what that lifetime across borders has brought to the page. For a book of this kind, another, more suitable way to categorize Faber's work must therefore be found.

I have chosen to divide up Faber's creations by 'world'. This is not form, but form is, perhaps, an ingredient. Mostly,

Faber's novels are unarguably novels. His poetry cannot be confused for anything else. His short stories usually exist within conventional formal boundaries. That said, any attempt to categorize Faber must embrace exceptions. One is the world of *The Crimson Petal*, which moves between the novel and the short-story forms, in two publications: the 900-page novel whose success transformed Faber's literary life, and *The Apple*, a slender complementary volume published four years later. These are so clearly part of the same *world* that it makes sense to group them together. The term 'world' is particularly useful for *The Crimson Petal* as it suggests commonalities, a set of rules and reader expectations, while allowing assessments to range across form and time period. They make for an uncommon, lopsided, but potent pair. Complicating things further, the author argues one story from *The Apple*, 'A Mighty Horde of Women in Very Big Hats, Advancing', '*is* a novel', despite its size (TA xviii). Worlds within worlds, then. Worlds, big and small. That too seems appropriate for Faber. The other key exception in terms of form is the 'novella'; as I will explore, Faber thinks of his prose fiction simply as short, medium-sized or long stories. Stories of similar word counts have, in different places, been labelled in different ways. I hope readers find the following structure a useful way to tackle what would otherwise be a hard-to-define body of work.

In this book I make a case for Faber as an artist whose writing across genre and form rewards deep critical engagement. His stories are marked out by their directness of tone, simplicity of language and playful mixing of genres, also by their sub-audible frequency, which concerns itself with the human urge to connect in spite of the often-elusive nature, as he sees it, of true connection. Alienation is a common trope, often seen through an outsider protagonist. Usually, a woman. Usually, in unfamiliar terrain. These concerns are explored in each chapter, with connective tissue between works identified. This book might be described as an interrogation of Faber's poetics of compassion, using examples from his earliest experiments right up to works in progress. Each chapter looks at case studies of Faber's work, with explorations of genre, literary approach and hybridity dealt with as part of the world in question. Though all are mentioned, not all Faber's major works are covered in depth.

INTRODUCTION

Chapter 1, 'Faber's World of the Short Story', focuses on the author's longstanding commitment to the form, in both realist and fantastic modes, as well as his trademark combination of both. His collections *Some Rain Must Fall* and *The Fahrenheit Twins* are discussed, drawing particularly on three case studies: 'Some Rain Must Fall', 'Fish' and 'Vanilla-Bright like Eminem'. Also, the author's journey in publishing. This latter element matters as the short story was, in practical terms, the way Faber's published writing life began.

In Chapter 2, 'Faber's World of the Novella (or Medium-Sized Story)', three fictions are covered: *The Hundred and Ninety-Nine Steps*, *The Courage Consort* and 'The Fahrenheit Twins'. Each of these three 'medium-sized stories' contains several key elements often found in the novella form. The nature of that distinctiveness is explored in this chapter. All three 'medium-sized stories' have been crowded out by other Faber works in terms of critical and commercial attention. All three deserve a more considered look.

Chapter 3, 'Faber's World of the Novel', uses three contrasting creations to assess Faber's development as a writer of compassionate fiction. It begins with a study of the unpublished early novel *A Photograph of Jesus* and Faber's history in the form, before interrogating his two most celebrated 'science fiction' novels, *Under the Skin* and *The Book of Strange New Things*. These two represent a major part of the reason for Faber's burgeoning international reputation; the first of these transformed the author's life.

Chapter 4, 'Faber's World of *The Crimson Petal*', interrogates the author's best-known novel alongside *The Apple*, its varied partner collection. The chapter analyses *The Crimson Petal*'s creative process, drawing upon previously unseen documents sent between writer, editor and publisher which are now in archives. A detailed narrative overview is also provided. The chapter then looks at Faber's reasoning for refusing to write a sequel and his preferring instead a collection of stories from the same world across time, a decision which confounded many fans of *The Crimson Petal* while delighting readers of his short fiction.

Chapter 5, 'Faber's World of Verse', addresses the author's singular volume of poetry. *Undying: A Love Story* is a world of its own, a book of autobiographical confessional poems about the illness and death of the author's wife Eva from cancer in 2014. For this book, it is appropriate to consider elements of his personal life Faber has chosen to make public, to illuminate understanding of the work. Alongside analysis of individual poems and biographical background, Faber's poetic approach is considered here, also what made him turn to the form.

Chapter 6, 'Faber, Out of Time', is a brief conclusion of sorts, considering how Faber's literary past, present and future are in continual exchange, reshaping each other over time. Subtitled 'A Look Back, A Look Forward', this explores Faber's unfinished and recent projects, several of which have been underway in various forms for many years.

Books in the Writers and Their Work series always introduce readers to the breadth and nature of a writer's body of work, and this one will do that. But it is not exclusively a skip through what is already in the public domain. Rather, it seeks to expand Faber Studies, drawing upon new, previously unseen documents such as unpublished fiction and the author's own short-story database, as well as email exchanges with the author and one of his editors. I have also utilized the University of Dundee's Canongate archive, which contains extensive correspondence, publisher material and editorial notes. This research informs the whole book, and I selectively quote from it.

Some books in this series focus on long-dead writers, others on living writers who do not engage in debates about their work. With *Michel Faber*, I believe this volume can be enhanced by including the writer in the conversation, as we often do in Creative Writing study. Throughout this book, I use the privilege of direct access to the author, still very much a relevant part of the contemporary literary landscape, to ask new questions. Faber is willing to engage with critical readings – as he wrote in the Foreword to *Michel Faber: Critical Essays*: 'Let me be un-British about this. I'm a serious artist and I write good books. They're enjoyable to read, but they reward study' (MFCE 1). Later in that Foreword, he acknowledged his view on his work is not the only valid one, seeing critical readings as a route to worthwhile illumination of elements that matter to the author but which are sometimes missed in reviews: 'the political, philosophical and aesthetic subtexts that academics identify in my books really do correspond to stuff I take great care to put in' (MFCE 2). He suggested he too benefitted from reading academic interrogations: 'To put it simply, we learn from each other' (MFCE 2). For me, the inclusion of primary research which engages with the author and those who work with him is an illustration of this mutual learning in action; I hope readers find it illuminating. The writer's voice is not the only one. Writers do not have exclusive insight regarding the works they have created. But they can be a valuable part of the conversation.

# 1

# Faber's World of the Short Story

For two reasons, the short story occupies an essential place in any conversation about Michel Faber's work. The first concerns the world of publishing: it was the short story that made Faber an acclaimed writer. The second relates to the ingredients his work contains. The following chapter explores both reasons, which demonstrate in different ways why any discussion of Faber's oeuvre must have short fiction as a primary focus. It interrogates Faber's first two collections and draws on case studies, contrasting in approach though similar in preoccupation. But first: some personal background allows us to trace the role the short story played in the young writer's development.

Michel Faber was born in the Netherlands in 1960 into a family of Dutch Baptists. He spent his early years on the country's western coast. His father had been a Nazi collaborator, and his mother had nearly starved in the winter of 1945. As Faber put it years later, 'You can imagine the guilt and horror that hung around in the atmosphere of our home.'[1] The child of a second marriage, he had an older half-brother and half-sister who, in their absence, play a part in the author's life story. In 1967, his parents moved to suburban Melbourne, Australia, though not everyone in the family got on the plane. Faber has described himself as a writer with 'a missing past',[2] and parts of his biography do remain firmly out of view. He describes his childhood and teenage years as 'inaccessible to me'.[3] This includes reading habits. (Aside from C. S. Lewis, whose prose style focused on the 'visceral and the palpable', Faber struggles to answer questions about his early literary influences.[4]) But he is a frank interviewee and has described his move and the associated break-up of the family unit as underlying much of his work – so much of it being about alienation, enforced separation and encounters with foreign cultures. During an on-stage interview with Thomas Oberender at the Internationales Literaturfestival Berlin, Faber was introduced as having moved to Australia with a brother. Faber corrected his host, then connected the fracture to his work:

> This is one of the things that probably lies beneath all my writing: My parents were very fucked up by World War II. They decided to leave the past behind them, and the past included their children from previous marriages. So they left those children behind in the Netherlands and emigrated to Australia just with me.[5]

Unsurprising, then, that the Dutch boy transplanted to Melbourne would grow up to write stories about characters somehow alien in their surroundings. After 1967, Faber did not see his brother for over a quarter of a century. He met his sister for the first time when she was 70. After joining an Australian school aged seven, knowing no English, on his first day young Michel 'stormed out of class vowing never to return'.[6] But he had to. Little wonder his narrators often experience some traumatic geographic displacement or schism that affects their understanding of the world, their new environment so unfamiliar as to seem otherworldly.

Young Michel starting writing at eight, in a mixture of Dutch and English. His first serious attempt at a short story, 'Knabbel and Babbel Go to the Moon', moved between the languages – the title suggests interplanetary travel was already an interest. By 1974 he was writing seriously, but at high school he retained a desire for privacy that would endure. Put bluntly, he was not the typical Aussie teenager. Faber is neurodivergent, which marked him out, as did his Dutch background and the fact that he was often busy 'writing novels, painting, [and] developing a passionate interest in avant-garde music'. Most of his school friends were girls and fellow pupils often assumed he was gay, a misconception he did not correct. As Faber wrote to his publisher decades later, in a rare, detailed autobiographical overview, 'Thus began a life-long interest in male/female sexual politics.' This letter makes clear how young Faber was when he settled on what he wanted to be: 'By the end of high school,' he wrote, 'I had no ambition to be anything other than a writer.'

In the same letter, he explained his reasons: 'Even then I was interested in in holding up a mirror to other people; challenging them morally and intellectually. I've come to think that literary fiction is the only forum for doing this without getting yourself beaten up and spat upon.'[7] Alongside his desire to write fiction, he continued to think about how also, one day, he might find a way to write meaningfully about music.

This singularity of ambition persisted through his time at the University of Melbourne, 'a sheer pleasure' during which Faber practised writing short stories and started writing and research for *The Crimson Petal*. After getting married in secret to Grayson Gerrard in his third year, 'in order for me to qualify for a TEAS (Tertiary Education Assistance Scheme) allowance', the two of them lived 'a life of poverty', during which time it 'never occurred to me that I would ever make a living from writing'. At this time, as Faber later told Jamie Byng, Head of Canongate, he 'held most published fiction in contempt and didn't want to be associated with it'. It was only later that he would lose this 'needless arrogance'. In the meantime, he wrote stories furiously but 'never submitted anything... I assumed history would take care of it somehow and besides, I was too poor – or too stingy – to spend the money on posting a manuscript.'[8]

After graduating, Faber spent several years in casual jobs, including cleaning work, then trained as a nurse, an occupation he stayed in for a decade. Though he consciously tried not to write about nursing, 'partly to preserve the privacy of my patients and partly because I wanted to train my readers (real or imagined) not to expect autobiographical material',[9] these experiences did train the young writer in compassion, empathy and consideration for the other. Stories begun in this period show an instinctive, deep-rooted affinity for the marginalized, the vulnerable, the powerless. As Faber told Byng years later, 'nursing taught me a lot about the rest of humanity'.

Faber's first marriage lasted ten years, but was in trouble after the first few. Grayson was English, originally from Winchester. She was also an aspiring writer, later an anthropologist. Photocopies of the typescript for her autobiographical unpublished novel were used by Faber to jot down 'plans and sketches for *The Crimson Petal*'.[10] The marriage included a six-week abortive attempt to emigrate to England in 1982.

Lacking a necessary stamp on his passport, Faber had to stay behind while Grayson flew back to Australia. He was stuck for a week in London, without funds, awaiting the next available flight. He knew his time spent homeless would be limited, but here he experienced a new kind of outsiderdom, which later influenced 'The Safehouse', one of his strongest stories, in which a man wakes up disorientated at the start of the tale, amid the stink of rubbish, desperate for shelter.

Eventually Faber would be back in the UK to stay, describing himself as being more comfortable in the northern hemisphere – he experienced intense migraines in Australia, 'triggered by bright sunlight'.[11] But for now he returned there, writing in his spare time as his first marriage broke down. By 1984, early drafts of key stories such as 'Fish' and 'Miss Fatt and Miss Thinne', for example, had been written, both of which explored the shock of profound loss in contrasting ways. While writing novels to his satisfaction proved a challenge for now, the size of the shorter form allowed Faber to get closer to completing works he was proud of. It also let him experiment across genre with what would become his three major modes: the fantastic, the mundane and a heady mixture of both.

In 1988, Faber met a woman called Eva Youren who quickly changed his life. His short fiction played a role in their relationship from the start, establishing the dynamic of the next 25 years. Writing in 2021 about 'Miss Fatt and Miss Thinne', Faber explained:

> This and 'Fish' were the two stories I read to Eva on the evening when we became lovers. I rented a room in the same shared household where she rented a room and we'd been growing friendlier over time but she was often away. She gathered that I was an unpublished writer and on this day she asked me to read her some of my stuff. She liked 'Fish' a lot but had some criticisms of 'Miss Fatt and Miss Thinne' and was fearless and uninhibited in expressing them. I thought 'This is the woman for me'.[12]

Eva was to become his greatest collaborator, editor and most credited support: most of his books are dedicated to her alone, perhaps in part because it was Eva who persuaded the young writer to let go of that arrogance and, with generosity of spirit, 'reach out to the readers "out there"'.[13]

In 1993, Faber moved across the world once more, this time with Eva and her family, taking his unpublished stories to Scotland. After they settled in a remote Highland village, he experienced significant 'periods of depression and mental fragility'.[14] As he has reflected since, 'I was so despairing and so distressed for so much of the 90s, convinced that I would end up possibly homeless or as some kind of fringe dweller.' He had been working in a care home 15 miles from his house, travelling by bike most of the time, spending part of his wages on taxis when the weather was poor. Then Eva pushed Michel to start submitting work, hopeful that moving his writing life forward might give him confidence. As he has said, 'I didn't get systematic about [sending out my work] until we were in Scotland and I was unemployed and she was supporting me.'[15] At this time, the novels might have been incomplete or unacceptable to the author, but several stories were carefully edited, and Eva was convinced of their distinctiveness.[16]

By this time, the key early story 'The Crust of Hell' was drafted. Described by Faber's future editor Judy Moir as being a 'strange and kind of funny' story about 'the adaptability of youth',[17] 'The Crust of Hell' suggested the coherence and quality of Faber's fiction was improving, but also hinted at the settings his stories would utilize in future, with extreme, contained, isolated landscapes a regular feature. In 'aggressively arid territory four hundred feet below sea level and half way between what could be called Africa and what could be called the Arab States' (SRMF 108), this story is set somewhere 'a map, unless you already know exactly where you are, is nothing but a pretty picture' (SRMF 109). Other examples of this approach include 'Sheep', set deep in the Scottish Highlands, at 'the alternative centre of the world', and 'The Fahrenheit Twins', set at 'the icy zenith' of the world (TFT 231). In Faber, extreme landscapes often apply pressure to the characters' situations, with natural and animal worlds acting in exchange with humanity. By the 1990s these areas of interest were well set, Faber's techniques and approaches being practised in an ongoing, vast series of fictional experiments.

As ever, Faber was working multiple stories at once, each of them documented in a private short-story database. Though the information here should not be treated as gospel – it was kept as a personal record, not intended as a resource for future biographers – it does document when stories were drafted and re-drafted, where they were submitted and who published or rejected these, in various forms. The database shows how full of rejection this period was; how even his most celebrated stories went unfinished for years or were rejected many times over, even by the smallest magazines, journals and competitions. In other words, how common Faber's experience was, compared to other aspiring writers.

Once he resolved to share his work, he pushed hard, and his three competition wins across 1996 and 1997 were very much the exception. Stories now lost, such as 'The Collar', were rejected multiple times, by places as diverse as BBC Radio 4 and the Phoenix Writers' Group Short Story Competition. The likes of 'Down the Up-Escalator in a Race Against Science' and 'The Highland Clearances' were submitted widely, never published. Many stories eventually published in *Some Rain Must Fall*, such as 'In Case of Vertigo', 'Nina's Hand', 'Pidgin American' and 'Sheep', had been turned down too. Studying this database now, it is hard to escape the conclusion that the floodgates had been flung open. With Eva's support, Faber was determined to find homes for his stories, somewhere, anywhere. This persistence, also the sheer volume of short fiction he was producing, has been somewhat lost. Newspaper and magazine interviews with Faber often briefly note the three competition wins alone, as if these were the only concessions this shy, resistant author ever made to the realities of the publishing world. Not so.

Rejections kept coming in the mid-1990s, but Eva's instincts about her husband's short fiction were well founded: now came the first of those three wins, 1996's St James Short Story Award for 'Some Rain Must Fall'. This was a key year, as he won the Macallan Short Story Award for 'Fish' as well; critically, he also successfully applied to the then-Scottish Arts Council for a small bursary. On the panel was Judy Moir, then working freelance. Twenty-five years later, Moir says: 'I remember being completely bowled over by his stories, particularly "Toy Story" – the extraordinary bravado of imagining God as a petulant, lonely child "playing" with the Earth, new lakes or fjords instantly created where he'd touched the planet.'[18] In 1997, Faber won the Highland-based Neil M. Gunn Award for

'Half a Million Pounds and a Miracle' too. The Macallan in particular, with a £6,000 prize, brought money, momentum, encouragement. Though none of this came with guarantees of further publication.

Moir played a crucial role here. After reading his stories on a panel alongside Jenny Brown, then the Scottish Arts Council's newly appointed Head of Literature, Moir recommended Faber send them to Canongate, an independent publisher in Edinburgh where she also worked sometimes. Faber was unknown, based far from any literary community, Edinburgh being some 200 miles south of the author's remote Highland home. He had no literary agent, no connections. Moir recommended Faber to Canongate Managing Director Jamie Byng, who 'whisked away' a 'huge package' of stories to consider with his then-assistant Emily Dewhurst. Soon Faber was offered a contract for a collection. Responding to Byng on 16th December 1997, Faber wrote: 'Your letter must rate as the most welcome piece of mail I've ever received in my life.'[19] In his excitement, the author suggested waiving a proposed £1,000 advance due on publication to 'help finance publicity and promotion'. Judy Moir was hired to work as editor on the book. She would soon join Canongate in the dual role of Editorial and Rights Manager, being Faber's editor for his first five books.

Sifting the original batch of stories was a significant task. By now, Faber had built up a large body of unpublished work, and he presented a full 60 stories to Canongate for consideration. After initial selections cut this down, Byng, Dewhurst and Moir sat around a table in early 1998 discussing potential selections, order and titles. (A printed summary, replete with marks out of 10, was headlined *Sheep and Other Stories*.) The author was involved in further selecting and ordering, while of 'the three Canongaters involved in the structural edit', Byng held sway. Aside from simply looking for quality, Moir remembers: 'we also wanted to showcase the range of [Faber's] imagination and voices, as well as the extraordinary spectrum regarding tone and setting'. Due to the sheer amount of submissions, some strong works were rejected: 'I recall being very touched by a story called "The Perfect W" and was sorry that it didn't make the final cut. (It was a story mostly about vaginal cosmetic surgery, which wasn't really a "thing" at that time!)'.[20] Cosmetic surgery and the alteration of bodies would be a crucial element of Faber's next manuscript.

When *Some Rain Must Fall* was published, it was critically well received, winning the Saltire Society's First Book of the Year prize in 1999, the author qualifying as 'Scottish by formation', beating Toni Davidson's cult classic *Scar Culture* to the prize. Meanwhile, there was further success at the Frankfurt Book Fair, a major publishing industry event. In her dual role, and one of three people at Canongate selling international rights at Frankfurt, Moir could help advocate for the book. Byng in particular was known as a brilliant salesman of his books. Moir remembers an initial offer from the French publisher 10:18, one of their editors displaying 'such excitement and enthusiasm that it spurred us on to sell that book in several languages'. Eichborn in Germany bought rights, as did Einaudi in Italy, Podium in the Netherlands and Harcourt in the US. All this was highly unusual. Moir remembers:

> It has always been extremely difficult to sell foreign rights for short stories, especially debut collections, so we were very proud of that achievement. Winning the Saltire First book award, simultaneously with an SAC [Scottish Arts Council] award, along with excellent reviews and prizes for individual stories helped us get interest from abroad.[21]

So Michel Faber was suddenly considered fast-rising, with offers rolling in for *Some Rain Must Fall* around the world. Meanwhile, he was busy writing *Under the Skin*, the novel which would soon eclipse these stories in terms of reception and interest, many future Faber readers having no interest in his short fiction at all. But this transformation would have been impossible without those early stories, which provided critical momentum, allowed for experimentation across genre and represented the beginning of his crucial long-term partnership with Canongate. Faber's approach to genre-hybridizing, form-hopping and determinedly uncommercial decision-making in future years would surely have tested the patience of all but the strongest of writer–publisher relationships. Those relationships are retained even now. They were built on the short story.

Many of these are as varied in concern and delivery as Faber's novels or 'medium-sized stories', so generalization is unwise. But it is fair to say that the short form has provided much more than simply a place in which to test out ideas and approaches later applied elsewhere, though there are commonalities readers may recognize that are evident in Faber's short fiction – the destabilizing of apparently 'real' and 'unreal' worlds, the religious undercurrents, the focus on connection or the search for it. Often his stories are daring, even shocking in subject matter. Elsewhere, they are playful with time and point of view. The styles and voices employed shift markedly. The best stories represent some of the author's most enduring literary contributions. Even if he had never written a novel, Faber's short works would be worth a volume of analysis on their own.

## *SOME RAIN MUST FALL*

As we have seen, Faber's first collection was written with no expectation of an audience – and the work itself shows little sign of writing for one. On the contrary, it reads like the work of someone entirely free of such considerations. Twenty-five years after initial UK publication, the appeal of *Some Rain Must Fall* remains partly because of its wide-ranging disrespect for genre boundaries, in its mix of fragmentary and more sustained pieces, also its determinedly transnational, morally conscious outlook.

Reading *Some Rain Must Fall* in order, two things stand out: first, the sheer variety of kinds of narrative experimented with, and second, the consistency of Faber's emotional territory: as he has written, 'one of the concerns that runs through all my work is the gulf which separates each human from all others and how valiantly we strive to cross it' (MFCE 2). That quotation is telling – even in facing down the impossibility of that gulf, the author names us as one: 'we', individuals engaged in that reaching out to connect. In *Some Rain Must Fall*, the author tests the limits of that reaching out utilizing a moral outlook. This leads him to search for possible connections between humans and non-humans, also humans, non-humans and their environments. These are nearly always fleeting. Sometimes, they are illusory. But they are often crucial to the narrative. In his essay 'House Full of Mouses: Genre, Language, and Creaturely Ethics', Timothy C. Baker notes:

> Faber's work challenges the fixity of species boundaries, and suggests the importance of reconsidering the relation between ethics and aesthetics when considering both humans and non-human animals. Looking at the relationship between language and the creaturely in Faber's work foregrounds the way he challenges not only literary genres, but the categorization of different forms of life. (MFCE 16)

As Baker explores, this challenge is plainly evident in Faber's short fiction, particularly in *Some Rain Must Fall* stories like 'Fish' and 'Sheep' – both stories named for animals.

As a collection, *Some Rain Must Fall* illustrates the many ways Faber's 'we' can manifest itself. It moves from the opening, titular story, in which the 'we' is the class of young children and their replacement teacher, bound together by tragedy though unknowing of each other's experience, to a supernatural world of horrors of a very different kind in 'Fish', where the 'we' is a mother, her daughter and the impossible shoal in the air. The 'we' in 'In Case of Vertigo' is Sister Jennifer and the bird at Suicide Point, an epiphanic moment where her fleeting illusion of connection to a creature overhead is taken as a message:

> God had given her yet another reason for living which she could pass onto others: the miracle of a bird in flight, the privilege of seeing a creature essentially different from oneself display its inhuman mastery, a display which one needed to be human and alive to witness and appreciate. It was necessary to keep living, if only to love the beauty of a bird, for birds themselves were incapable of loving it. (SRMF 32)

In some Faber stories, animal perceives human; here, human perceives animal. In both cases, perception is full of subjectivity, misunderstanding – neither can bridge the unbridgeable gulf – but they still form part of a 'we' the author keeps returning to.

In 'Toy Story', the tale that so stood out to Judy Moir, the 'we' is a child-God and the abandoned planet Earth he plays in. Much of the planet stays frustratingly untouchable, though voices inside that world reach his ears, 'full of love and longing and reaching for the impossible' (SRMF 41). The conceit here, also in 'Sheep', is to take a common perspective and invert it, a pattern noted in the *Publisher's Weekly* review of *Some Rain Must Fall* at the time of publication, though less noticed perhaps were Faber's representations of environment. As seen by the child-God full of wonder, the environment stands in for what is human or animal in other stories – Earth remains shrouded in mystery, even to God: 'his eyes would goggle with the strange new things he found there' (SRMF 36):

> It was all fog, really, like a haze of tiredness over God's eyes. As for hurricanes, tornadoes, lightning, hail, falling snow, even rain: these were phenomena he would never see, no matter how intently he squinted. For, when there were clouds in the sky, they hid these spectacular sights from him; when there were no clouds, these sights did not exist to be seen.
>
> The first time God realised this, perched on his wobbly chair in the middle of the room, he was sickened by how perfectly he was excluded, and hung his head. (SRMF 38)

In Faber's short fiction, even gods remain in isolation, despite their best efforts. Late in 'Toy Story', God tries to communicate with the people of Earth, though he cannot be heard. The story ends with God dreaming of another child like him being within reach. In 'an ecstasy of loneliness', he dreams of running 'all night, forever and ever, until, in the morning, he woke, remembering nothing, except that it had been good, and he was happy' (SRMF 42).

The second half of the collection switches modes repeatedly, experimenting with voices, dialects, genders and registers, also typography and page layout. In 'Miss Fatt and Miss Thinne', 'physicalities are important' (SRMF 43). The 'we' here is two women who continue to reach for each other even as they surrender to their respective tragicomic physical conditions, one losing weight to an alarming degree while the other puts it on. Increasingly separated from each other as if divided into liquid and solid, they are unable to understand what the other has lived through, though they comfort each other to the last anyway, with desperate tenderness.

In 'Somewhere Warm and Comfortable', the reaching 'we' is a pair of boy–girl siblings, the girl hiding her abortion from their mother. This is an understated, affecting, realist two-hander, which shows how Faber's characters attempt to understand each other. Brother Scott cannot know the physical and emotional anguish his sister Christine is going through, determined as she is to find 'somewhere warm and comfortable' to suffer in secret; she cannot understand his confusion and embarrassment, uncomfortable as he is with a stolen magazine hidden in his trousers. Christine rests on Scott's lap, the gap between the two of them undeniable, the connection too:

> 'Chris?' he ventured, shaking her gently.
>
> 'Leave me alone,' she slurred. 'Stay with me.' (SRMF 89)

Next is 'Nina's Hand', a study in unfamiliarity in the 'world of things beyond the physical' (SRMF 95). The hand has a mind of its own, though woman and hand are presented from the outset like a couple in trouble: 'The last night they slept together, Nina's right hand nestled under her pillow, as if seeking to stroke her face' (SRMF 93). Stories such as 'Nina's Hand' and 'Somewhere Warm and Comfortable' may seem like they must have been written by different authors. But consider them as short exercises in the possibilities and limits of connection, and a through-line becomes clear.

Towards the end of the collection, several longer stories explore the potential for common ground in uncommon settings. 'Pidgin American' tells the story of Polish Katarzyna, 'doing London' (SRMF 161). By day, she waitresses at her uncle's restaurant where she is harassed by customers; by night, she samples the clubbing scene and sleeps with strange men (SRMF 161). Meanwhile, 'The Tunnel of Love', featuring a rare male protagonist, is a meditation on love set in and around a pornography shop. Asked about communication in his short fiction many years after *Some Rain Must Fall*, Faber reflected:

> The pointlessness and inefficacy of 'communication' is one of the recurrent themes in my work. People fundamentally misunderstand each other, often without even recognising that their vocalisations are meaningless to the other person. Karen articulates this perception very well in 'The Tunnel of Love'. Humans are just animals. They need animal things from each other and language (in evolutionary terms) is just a belated add-on.[22]

Seen this way, 'The Tunnel of Love' is of a piece with the other stories in *Some Rain Must Fall*. It is a disparate collection, but also coherent. Many of these stories display not just the diversity of approach to genre Faber is now known for, but also his approach to harnessing empathy as a defining feature in his fiction, in spite of language's limitations. The following two case studies show how that works in more detail.

## 'Some Rain Must Fall'

Given that Faber's fiction is so concerned with efforts to bridge the gulf between beings, it is interesting that the first story in his debut book opens with one character trying to reach out for his partner, in vain. In the opening lines of 'Some Rain Must Fall', readers sense an immediate tension:

> Frances Strathairn came home to find that her partner had cooked her a meal.
>
> 'First day at your new job,' he said. 'I thought you'd be exhausted.'
>
> *My relationship with this man is in crisis,* Frances reminded herself, kissing him on the lips. *There is no doubt about it.*
>
> But of course there was doubt. Exhausted, she collapsed on the sofa and ate her meal, which was excellent. Her own recipe, followed to perfection. (SRMF 1)

Immediately the dynamics of this relationship are clear. Frances's partner's kindness cannot be denied. The meal's timing and execution show thoughtfulness, consideration for her needs. But these truths cannot disguise another need that haunts the story to come. The repetition of the word 'exhausted' is indicative. Frances is too tired to face the crisis, so the crisis grows. The chances of this relationship surviving are slim.

After this brief relationship sketch, Faber starts the story afresh, beginning with Frances's experience with her new class of primary-school children: 'The first thing she'd got them to do was tidy up' (SRMF 1). She asks them to do this not because tidiness matters to her, but because this is 'what the children craved'. She has suddenly replaced another teacher. The children's vulnerability is hinted at: 'They needed to demonstrate their goodness, their usefulness; they needed her to demonstrate her authority. Most of all, they needed life to go on, with a minimum of fuss.' The author seeds that some terrible trauma has taken place before Frances's arrival. She is paid three times as much as other teachers, but why? Small clues hide within mundane mini-scenes. Pencil cases are not emptied, they are 'disembowelled' (SRMF 2). The class's previous teacher is described as having 'lost her head' by Fiona, one of the children (SRMF 4). The story continues chronologically, moving between the classroom and Frances in her village home. Hints keep coming. Frances's partner, Nick, accepts that they sleep separately – 'well-behaved, well-behaved, well-behaved,' she complains. She longs for him to 'knock her off course, or at least dare to try' (SRMF 4). The course in the classroom is clear: Frances must assess the children in her care, giving them what they need. Though as with so many Faber characters, Frances cannot possibly understand what they have been through.

One way she tries to do this is through text itself. As we shall see, a recurring trope of Michel Faber's short fiction is the use of the epistolary form. From the letter of complaint in 'Tabitha Warren', to Margo's letters to NASA in 'Accountability', to the text on t-shirts of the lost souls in 'The Safehouse', Faber has often returned to letters, diaries, reports and to texts within texts as a way to demonstrate that gulf between characters, also to explore attempts to bridge it. Interesting, then, that the epistolary plays such an essential part in the titular story in Faber's first collection.

In the second part of 'Some Rain Must Fall', Frances reads a selection of essays written by the pupils, giving readers their voices, unfiltered. These children have had very different experiences. One, who missed the crucial day with food poisoning, turns on the charm for her new teacher, Mrs MacShane having 'simply disappeared from her young life as if rubbed out by that lovely new eraser' (SRMF 5). Another child covered his eyes out of embarrassment at the key moment. Another writes a single-line essay: 'The school is fine and my old teacher is fine' (SRMF 6). Frances thinks about these essays while having sex, her worlds of home and school intertwined. She will push Nick away, but tells him to come to her. She credits him with perceptiveness when it comes to strangers, though he cannot see the truth of their relationship. These twin tensions – of what is really going on at home and at school – are critical to the story's effectiveness. Tensions work with, not against, each other.

Like many Faber protagonists, Frances is complex. At work, she thrives: 'her talent was to radiate safety and the restoration of order' (SRMF 8), safety and order being two elements she resents in her personal life. She genuinely worries for the children, she cares for them, seemingly effortless in her ability to adapt to the needs of the community she has been charged with. That community follows Frances's instructions together in class, though the children, like the adults, are hiding: '*My old teacher is fine and everything els is to* [sic],' insists Tommy Munro, echoing his classmate Greg Barre (SRMF 9). But Tommy is struggling with ruling straight margins, 'his emotions corkscrewed deep into his pigeon chest'. Faber increasingly intercuts classroom events with class essays, revealing the awful truth. By the time it arrives, readers see the class not as a singular mass but as a loose collection of vulnerable individuals, desperate for reassurance. Frances also looks for reassurance in her argument with Nick, who will not commit to having children. Even in his aggression, Nick is vulnerable too. In Faber, this story shows, everyone is.

Frances and Nick have moved before. As in Exeter, Belfast too, Frances's job is to go wherever tragedy is, this one being that teacher Mrs MacShane was murdered by her husband in front of the whole class. This horrifying scene is finally glimpsed late in the story through the eyes of Katie Rusek, a girl shown catching 'the devolution of responsibility as if it were a basketball' when class crises break out like a rash (SRMF 16). Katie describes the murder graphically in her essay, but it is her final reflection that stands out: 'Every time I think about that day I feel sick. I ask myself, will I ever get over it?' (SRMF 17). Katie does not know yet, but Frances is due to move to the next aftermath soon. The impact on those left behind is ongoing.

This serves to further undermine what some readers may feel is the only thing they can be sure of so far: that Frances is doing right by these children. The story closes with her talking 'on and on' to them, making up a heart-warming tale about her and her husband repairing to the Rotheray Hotel because of recent rains (she and Nick are not married, never will be). She tells the children she could manage the strain she was under 'because she had people to help her, and soon everything would return to normal' (SRMF 17). Readers are encouraged to recognize the value of that reassurance, also its limits. Frances soothes and supports the children, as she will support the new teacher, due soon. In the final lines, a crying child, Jacqui, repositions herself 'in the hollow of Frances's breast, reconnecting with her heartbeat' (SRMF 18), as she tells her: 'Everything will be alright.' The rest of the story suggests otherwise.

## 'Fish'

As the first story in this collection ends with a woman comforting a young girl, so the second starts with the same thing, in a different context: 'It wasn't what child psychologists would have said was best, but there weren't any child psychologists anymore, and her daughter needed help just the same' (SRMF 19). 'Some Rain Must Fall' takes place in a familiar world. 'Fish' does not.

In the room where Janet and her daughter Kif Kif sleep, flywire stretches 'taut from floor to ceiling, the support struts and entrance zipper glowing in the candlelight' (SRMF 19). A tick-tick-ticking goes unexplained. Janet worries something might be 'eating through the wire'. Readers see through Janet's eyes as Kif Kif sleeps. What she observes through the darkness is familiar to her – 30 or 40 little fish, 'hovering in the air, bumbling against the flywire, trying to get in'. If this is an attack, it is a strange one. Janet lights a cigar and the fish scatter. These 'shining little bodies' head off in different directions, unseeing, bumping into things in the room, before being drawn back to the flywire. Like Frances in 'Some Rain Must Fall', Janet seeks to reassure the child, powerless as she is to deny their shared reality: '"It's all right, darling," murmured Janet, stroking her through the blankets. "Nothing to be afraid of"' (SRMF 20). But there is.

The following morning, mother and daughter brave the outside, walking through the 'gaping and dead' fish that litter the ground. Typically for Faber's fantastic stories, the rules of their world go unexplained, with occasional evidence littered for readers as they go, using brief flashbacks as a narrative device. In one case, the trauma of the day when their house has been broken into, the graffiti slogan of the Church of Armageddon

– 'THE FIRST SHALL BE LAST!' – thrust into the relative peace of the present. Janet and Kif Kif lock the door behind them, though even the volume of the locking is troubling: 'sound was so much louder these days than it had sounded in the days when there were things like cars, factories and people running' (SRMF 21). But the fish make no noise. In their millions they fill the air; barracuda sweeping 'without warning in and out of broken windows'; starfish wriggling 'on the bonnets of rusty cars'; octopi cartwheeling 'in slow motion through the air'. This picture is all the more nightmarish for the fact that '[e]ven the open-mouthed shriek of a shark attack would be obscenely silent, so there was actually no point in keeping your ears cocked, though you always did' (SRMF 21). Food is scarce. Mother and daughter must be careful. But of what? Faber continues to puncture the present moment of the story – mother and daughter zigzagging through the streets, on the lookout – with speculative commentary. Readers must do most of the work themselves.

Imagery throughout is vivid and discombobulating. Graffiti provides the strongest clues to the rules of this reality: 'ANY CRETURE THAT CAN READ THIS, YOU'RE DAYS ARE NUMBERED! [sic]' (SRMF 22). 'LET THE DRY LAND DISAPPEAR!' (SRMF 23). Janet and Kif Kif go to the soup kitchen, then return home. Increasingly, the narrative is overtaken by Janet's internal monologue. She contemplates the fact that her daughter has 'never smelled air untainted by decay' (SRMF 23). She agrees with the Army: 'the world was no longer intended for human beings'. Yet here they are, stuck in it. Janet is jolted out of her brooding by several blue-black killer whales 'emerging from the low grey clouds', hanging huge in the sky 'like black zeppelins' (SRMF 24). The whales are heading towards our protagonists. At first, it seems one of them will reach them. Then it smashes into an old building instead, as if on purpose, followed by its fellow whales.

The final page of this dense eight-page story bears repeated readings, so subtle is its implication. Like Frances and Nick's initial meal in 'Some Rain Must Fall', the same event is experienced in ways so different that it seems like the two characters are on different planets. Janet's response to the shock of this realization regarding the whales is to turn inward, reminding herself of why she must keep going:

> She wasn't really very grateful to be alive; life had been conceded too far beyond the extremity of terror. To be unconscious in the long gullet of a whale: that would have been *real* mercy, not this ghastly approximation of survival. Only, she must *pretend* to be alive, *pretend* to have hope, spirit, feeling, for the sake of her daughter, so that her daughter wouldn't give up. She must be strong for her daughter, comfort her, get her home to bed, carry her there if need be. (SRMF 25)

Here, Faber provides a moment of apparent clarity, only to undercut it. Where Janet experiences that 'attenuated minute the whales circled the ruin' as a kind of hell, symbolic of their impossible situation, her daughter, born into this strange new world, finds it exhilarating. Tellingly, Janet's realization comes directly after her meditation on what it might be like to be swallowed by a whale. No sooner is she sure of her place than she is shaken from it, turning on Kif Kif when she realizes her daughter's expression is 'radiant' at the sight of this destruction. Kif Kif describes the scene as 'amazing' and Janet is furious, shaking, hitting her child, helpless in the face of undeniable evidence that they see their reality differently. But even now, mother and daughter are not safe:

'Come on!' shouted the panting child, crossly. 'Stupid!'

Janet stumbled along, stumbling partly because she was too tall to be led properly by a six-year-old. She glanced over her shoulder to see what the child had already spotted: a school of moray eel gathering twenty yards away, attracted by the commotion of the fight and the smell of human flesh.

> Janet gained her stride, scooped up her unprotesting daughter in her arms and ran and ran. (SRMF 26)

In turning on each other, Janet and Kif Kif have revealed themselves to potential attackers on the lookout for human food. They must flee.

The story finishes as it started, in closeness, mother and daughter within the confines of the temporary safety they find behind the flywire. Janet lies about the root of her anger, the distance between them still undeniable, though they are a society of two, stuck with each other. This distance is reinforced in the story's final line, in which a sleepy Kif Kif claims, vaguely, that she is not scared of big fish: "'I have nightmares about other stuff," she said' (SRMF 26). The story opened with Janet speculating over the root of her daughter's fears. The subsequent drama has only made her less sure, their distance undeniable. Faber's characters attempt to bridge gaps right across his oeuvre, though as the author acknowledges, these two case studies are illustrative of what was to come, both in this collection and in the author's future books:

> The related underlying themes of 'Some Rain Must Fall' and 'Fish' are an indication, right at the start of my publication history, that the Michel Faber range of concerns is not actually that broad. What makes my work seem so various is the range of approaches, genres, tones, characterisations and techniques. I build radically different universes each time and I don't have a comfort zone. Maybe on some level I'm trying to make sure that the reader doesn't feel they're getting the same old thing yet again – 'Here's Michel Faber writing about loss and resilience and alienation as per usual'.[23]

The author's sense of self-awareness is acute, his range of concerns narrow indeed. What makes his work remarkable is not the *idea* of exploring similar territory in multiple genres and contexts, but the *ability* to render these convincingly. That ability is evidenced right across *Some Rain Must Fall*.

## THE FAHRENHEIT TWINS

By the time Michel Faber's second collection, *The Fahrenheit Twins*, was published in 2005, the author's life was unrecognisable compared to when *Some Rain Must Fall* appeared seven years earlier. Now he was a bestselling author, translated into 25 languages, with two critically acclaimed novels published around the world. Readers of those books had expectations of his work, expectations very much undermined by *The Fahrenheit Twins*, 'a collection of weird tales'[24] every bit as diverse, disorientating and fabulous as its short fiction predecessor. Published in the US as *Vanilla Bright like Eminem*, though without the titular story from the UK edition (and with the hyphen dropped between 'Vanilla' and 'Bright'), this collection contains several of Faber's finest works. *The Fahrenheit Twins* was generally received well and served to reinforce Faber's reputation, also encouraging more academic interrogations of his oeuvre – though naturally, it found a smaller readership than the novels. It might have been shorter (it contains 17 stories); some critics noted unevenness in quality. But in several key pieces, Faber showed he was able to find new ways to explore that 'narrow territory', imagining more new worlds where connection remains elusive, understanding just out of reach.

'The Safehouse' in particular shows this. In its sensitively rendered first-person perspective on disconnectedness among those who society has cast aside, the story follows one man as he discovers the shelter where he will be cared for (but where he cannot appreciate the tragedies of those around him). This story is almost comically, quintessentially Faber-esque in its concerns. That said, its central conceit is dealt with deftly. People in this world must wear t-shirts detailing who they have become estranged from, t-shirts written partially in mathematical code denoting various tragedies and abuses, t-shirts they are not allowed to remove or read. The delivery is powerful, the narrative surprising in its twists and turns. Loss, resilience and alienation all feature. Once again, the power of written text is central.

Multiple reviewers picked 'The Safehouse' as being the standout story here, along with 'The Eyes of the Soul', 'Tabitha Warren', also 'The Fahrenheit Twins' itself. This last example is the focus of a case study in Chapter 2, being one of Faber's 'medium-sized stories'. But for our final short fiction case study we turn to an unusually mundane setting, as far as Faber stories go, chosen because of the way it approaches time.

### 'Vanilla-Bright like Eminem'

'Vanilla-Bright like Eminem' traces the happiest moment of an American father's life. It takes place on a train during a holiday in Scotland, though, Alice Munro-like, it sweeps forward and back in time by many years to charge that train journey with the emotional weight of the family's experience in the distant past and future.

It is worth pausing on Munro for a moment. Famously, Faber rarely reads fiction, preferring music and comics to prose forms (he is also an illustrator). He has not been influenced by the great

Canadian short-story writer, and cannot remember having read her work before Eva introduced him to it (she was a big fan).[25] But there is a relevant commonality of approach here that some close readers may notice. Ailsa Cox's book *Alice Munro* is both a study of one writer and a study in the short form itself. In her Introduction, she writes: 'For Munro, storytelling is not a linear process. It is more like exploring a house than wandering down a straight road.'[26] In a chapter on epiphanies and intuitions, Cox explores what she calls the short story's 'ability to engage with the passing moment'.[27] Faber's approach to epiphanies and intuitions is sometimes similar to Munro's.

In numerous Faber stories, a moment is presented initially before the house of that moment is explored in all its nuance, doubt and complexity as the story progresses. This makes for fiction that appears to meander through past, present and sometimes future but is carefully constructed, leaving readers to contemplate the nature of that passing moment for the characters involved and the reader too. 'Vanilla-Bright like Eminem' represents the best example of this in action; it is certainly one of Faber's most widely read and oft-studied stories. Its opening lines focus on a train journey. It starts as if suspended in a fragment of time, when our protagonist is worried he might drift off:

> Don, son of people no longer living, husband of Alice, father of Drew and Aleesha, is very, very close to experiencing the happiest moment of his life.
>
> It's 10.03 according to his watch, and he is travelling down through the Scottish Highlands to Inverness, tired and ever-so-slightly anxious in case he falls asleep between now and when the train reaches the station, and misses his cue to say to Alice, Drew and Aleesha, 'Ok, this is Inverness. Let's move it.' (TFT 223)

The reader's perspective on this almost-moment will be ever-shifting as new evidence is presented, new context explored. But the narrative will keep coming back to Don and his family, on the train. That return helps to anchor a tale that might otherwise seem to drift.

After this initial introduction, the narrator turns to the members of Don's immediate family, comparing them to the locals and each other. Fifteen-year-old Drew is big, like his father: '[b]oth of them have hands like boxers'. Quickly the narrative slips from the present, as if it cannot stand on its own, with tasters of moments leading up to the train journey hinted at or quoted from. Readers learn that three hours ago, Drew and his dad argued. Both Aleesha, 13, and 40-year-old Alice, are sleeping. Amid this description of the present, doubt is seeded about the life this family leads outside of the train. Alice's habit of complaining about her body; Don's fumbling attempts to work out what she wants him to say in response. Then the story segues into the moment that – before the one he's about to have – has *until now* been the happiest moment in Don's life. This took place many years earlier, outside a Kentucky Fried Chicken, Don and Alice sure they would soon make love. It is not the lovemaking nor the three days in bed he remembers vividly, but 'her smile when he approached her – that smile of welcome and anticipation and conviction that she was doing the right thing' (TFT 225).

As the train progresses towards Inverness, the present is increasingly crowded out by the memories that intrude on Don's sleepy mind. Arguments with the kids about whether to visit the Louvre or Eurodisney one year. The way Aleesha unknowingly disturbed him with evidence of her 'maturing sexuality' as she innocently, playfully reached into the pocket of his military pants. Also, the arguments about Drew's new Eminem-style bleached-blonde mop, Don horrified by his son 'pledging fellowship with ghetto youth' when he was really a 'white kid living with his folks in the suburbs of West Springfield, with a holiday to Scotland on the horizon'. These fights, replaying in Don's mind on the train, have been made fiercer by Drew's defence: 'it's my hair, and my money' (TFT 226).

By this point, Don is far from the happiness announced as within reach at the start of the story. He is also, in a sense, far from the train to Inverness, deep into the detail of these past disputes, which have spiralled in advance of this holiday. The fight is not just about hair. The widening gulf between the generations of this family is inescapable, and terrifying to all. And yet fleeting moments provide solace, even if they go misunderstood. Aleesha wakes for a moment, smiling at her father. He cannot know why, but he smiles in return. This is the cue for the arrival of the longed-for moment.

The moment is so small that no one else sees it; even those involved might find its impact curious. Aleesha reaches for her brother across the aisle of the train carriage, comb in her hand. The ordinary is made extraordinary through attention to detail. As Don experiences it, time seems elastic, the familiar suddenly unfamiliar:

> Carefully, oh-so-slowly, she runs the teeth of her comb through her brother's hair. Time slows right down. The comb lifts the nap of Drew's crop, revealing rich brown roots under the bleached exterior. The way it lifts and resettles is mesmerizing, like watching wheat being rustled by the breeze.
>
> Drew doesn't stir; he's either deeply asleep or determined to ignore his sister. She combs on, tenderly, aware of her dad watching her, aware of the spell she's casting over him. Drew's hair lifts and re-settles, lifts and re-settles, the bristles soft as a brand-new paintbrush...

In Faber, when something is made ridiculous, there is a good chance that judgement, wherever it comes from, will be undermined. Here, language moves from the prosaic to the poetic: ultimately, despite his reservations, Don ends up speculating this may be 'the best haircut in the world'. Through repetition, the use of peaceful imagery and with minute attention to detail, the swirl of memories morphs into focus on the movement of a comb through a sleeping teenager's hair. But all moments pass. Eventually, Don becomes distracted once more. By a glimpse of his wife's naked flesh. By how he still wants her. Briefly, his attention returns to the poetry of Aleesha and the comb – she is still combing, even now, through Drew's unimprovable hair. *This* is the happiest moment in Don's life.

Next, the narrator moves into the future, showing readers what Don cannot yet see. Like a train picking up speed, the pace increases so readers get ever-faster glimpses of the family's future – Aleesha announcing a change to her name (she's Ellen now); Aleesha's abortion, which alters her smile forever; her future engagement and pregnancy by a man who 'adores her'. After that, the pace seems to run almost out of control, that high-speed swirl all the story has become. Drew, in South America, distant and unreachable, working construction sites in 'what look like shanty towns' (TFT 229). Alice's stiff walk, the first evidence of the illness that will kill her – Faber moves through her decline and death in two lines – before Don says he won't love again. He does though; in old age, he is happily remarried.

In Faber's short fiction, certainty is usually revealed to be folly. This is evident, for example, in the first lines of 'The Safehouse': 'I wake up, blinking hard against the sky, and the first thing I remember is that my wife cannot forgive me. Never, ever. Then I remind myself I don't have a wife anymore' (TFT 1). Here, too. 'Vanilla-Bright like Eminem' ends with the following lines, poetic repetition used to heighten the senses and increase narrative tension, finally bringing readers back to the train:

> ...she'll make him happy [Don's second wife], happier than he ever expected to be in his old age, happier than any of the other miserable old coots that live in his neighbourhood, happier than he's ever been in fact, except for may be a couple of isolated moments, like the smile of a young woman waiting to be his lover, her face glowing in the light of a fast food franchise, and like the hand of his daughter floating above the head of his son, on this morning in a Scottish train, the haircut making everything worthwhile, shining so bright it leaves a pattern on your retina when you close your eyes, vanilla-bright like Eminem. (TFT 230)

This family, who grow, fight, die, drift apart – who fellow passengers might see as typical American tourists – are rendered, through Don's experience, with compassion, respect and nuance. They can be laughed at, momentarily, as we all can be, but there are few cartoons in Faber. The way language is selected, the narrative swirl delivered, means readers have little choice but to empathize with this family. As they must with the deceased author in 'Tabitha Warren'. As they must with Christine in 'The Smallness of the Action', though she attacks her baby. As they must with Gail in 'Serious Swimmers', though her heroin addiction has led to familial estrangement. The science fiction and fantasy pioneer M. John Harrison wrote in his review of *The Fahrenheit Twins* that Faber's second collection is a study in fracture and its consequences – consequences readers are encouraged to empathize with. In Faber, he writes, '[f]ragility is universal... No one is as whole as they seem.'[28]

# 2

# Faber's World of the Novella (or Medium-Sized Story)

There is no universally accepted definition of the novella, though few dispute that the form originated in Italy in the Middle Ages; agreement is also widespread that it influenced the development of the short-story and novel forms in Europe. But what exactly constitutes a novella? Some definitions suggest word count is critical: contemporary competitions range from 10,000 to 50,000 as a defining feature, though generalization is limiting, and there is a significant difference between the possibilities of a 10,000 and a 50,000-word fiction. Word count aside, most novellas have several key elements in common: a tight narrative focus, a small cast and a singular geographical setting. In a 2012 *New Yorker* article, 'Notes on the Novella', the novelist Ian McEwan reached for a description of the unique pressures applied by the form:

> ...the demands of economy push writers to polish their sentences to precision and clarity, to bring off their effects with unusual intensity, to remain focussed on the point of their creation and drive it forward with functional single-mindedness, and to end it with a mind to its unity. They don't ramble or preach, they spare us their quintuple subplots and swollen midsections.[1]

The strength of Michel Faber's novellas in particular lies in that 'functional single-mindedness', that 'unity' which comes from narrowly controlled structural decision-making. In novels like *The Crimson Petal*, those 'quintuple subplots and swollen midsections' are a strength. But Faber's novellas display an ability to resist such temptations, retaining that singular focus, also a sense that the story is being pulled along without getting distracted by other, related narratives. But what counts as a Faber novella? And does the term matter?

The author says the word 'novella' means nothing to him. For Faber, there are simply *stories*, and each of those is *the size it needs to be*, something only discoverable in the making. The term 'novella' is used by publishers and critics, and the author is neither. Rather, for works which are neither short nor long, he prefers the understated term 'medium-sized'. Across his literary life, some of these stories have been published as short stories, others as novellas. On occasion some have been published as both, in different contexts, causing confusion.

For this book, I considered whether to use the term 'novella' at all; ultimately I decided it remains useful, as a way to read our three case studies. But the term 'medium-sized story' is also useful, allowing this chapter to interrogate comparable fictions, all of which can be honestly called 'medium-sized'. As it happens, they also have traits typical of novellas. I will not attempt to cover all Faber's medium-sized stories here – *The Fire Gospel*, for instance, was published as part of the sprawling, international series The Myths in 2008, and was promoted as a novella. Instead, I focus on just three case studies: *The Hundred and Ninety-Nine Steps*, *The Courage Consort* and *The Fahrenheit Twins* (the novella, rather than the short-story collection).

The last of these is the hardest to categorize. Drafted in 1998, considered briefly for inclusion in *Some Rain Must Fall*, then published in the US, alongside *The Hundred and Ninety-Nine Steps* and *The Courage Consort*, in a single volume titled *The Courage Consort: Three Novellas*, it finally became the titular story in the UK edition of Faber's second short-story collection. Despite a strange genesis, then, it has history with the other case studies in this chapter. Though radically different in setting and genre, they each feature common Faber preoccupations. All three contain focused, singular narratives. They all have small casts. All are set primarily in one location.

## THE HUNDRED AND NINETY-NINE STEPS

In a sign of the porous boundary between the two forms, Michel Faber's first published 'novella' was supposed to be a short story. Set in and around the 1,500-year-old Whitby Abbey in North Yorkshire, it came about because Keith Wilson, the Abbey's artist-in-residence in the year 2000, invited Faber to write a story about the English Heritage dig happening there. This was an early example of Faber's burgeoning reputation leading to surprising commissions. A pattern was emerging, in which Faber was being increasingly seen as a rising 'Scottish', or sometimes 'British', writer who specialized in the Gothic, the animal, the environmental. *The Hundred and Ninety-Nine Steps* contains elements of all three.

With the Whitby commission, Faber did comply with the request, though he moved beyond the Heritage dig, the ancient ruins acting more as atmospheric backdrop than primary focus. Faber wrote *The Hundred and Ninety-Nine Steps* after Wilson took him and Eva on guided tours of Whitby. Knowing little about the place, the author needed help to make its past and present convincing. (In 2000, he was also researching *The Crimson Petal*, so was getting used to consulting with specialists.) Wilson put him in touch with an archaeologist, a paper conservator, also the Whitby Literary and Philosophical Society. The more Faber researched, the more his piece grew. Soon, it was large enough to stand alone. After the initial success of *Under the Skin*, Canongate wanted to know: did Faber have any other unpublished work? 'We were desperate to have anything from him,' remembers Judy Moir.[2] Soon her old university professor was providing research advice for *The Hundred and Ninety-Nine Steps*. Type large and margins thick, it was scheduled for release quickly. Eva's photographs from the Whitby trip were peppered throughout the hardback.[3]

As noted in the *Sunday Herald* review of the time, *The Hundred and Ninety-Nine Steps* is an attempt to meld several distinct literary traditions: that of the ghost story, the historical thriller and the Gothic romance,[4] knowingly utilizing tropes from these while undermining genre expectations. All this is situated in a deceptively simple, typically Faber-esque narrative about the search for connection. In this case, the connection is pursued across time, something several positive reviews picked up on. Can those in the present gain meaningful access to the souls of history? Can the dead reach into the present? The book's epigraph, from Tennyson, suggests literature itself may have that power: 'So word by word, and line by line/The dead man touch'd me from the past.' The word 'touch' stands out. For protagonist Siân, as the *Evening Standard* review noted, it acts as a haunting across time: 'With impressive subtlety and economy, Faber raises questions about... the way in which the past haunts the present and the invisible undercurrents lying beneath human relations.'

*The Hundred and Ninety-Nine Steps* collapses time repeatedly, swimming between the 7th century (when Abbess Hild founded the monastery in Whitby), the 18th century (when the story's found text was written) and the 21st century (Siân's present, in Whitby). There are also regular reflections on Siân's time in 1990s wartime Bosnia. Faber uses Whitby, its past ever-present through both its people and places, to craft a story that at once feels contemporary and historic, realist and fantastic too.

The book's title refers to the steps connecting the modern Abbey to the ruins of the past, steps characters keep returning to like a chorus as the story progresses; it is also a nod to John Buchan's classic Scottish novel *The Thirty-Nine Steps*. Where Buchan's thriller featured an archetypal man-on-the-run, Faber's text is more of a meditation on the possibility of a different kind of escape, exploring the relationship between the emotional ruins of the present and the physical ruins of the past. Throughout, Faber utilizes his preferred epistolary technique, bringing characters to life by giving them direct voice in their written texts. Juxtaposing the 18th and 21st centuries in particular, Faber offers glimpses into the lives of long-dead characters who cannot be fully understood, by the protagonist or anyone else.

The narrative of *The Hundred and Ninety-Nine Steps* follows Siân, a lonely woman in her thirties who comes to Whitby to work on the dig and try to forget her past. By day, Siân sifts for fragments of skeletons. By night, she suffers from terrible visions. With a familiar trope from Gothic horror, she imagines 'being first seduced, then murdered', repeatedly. Readers learn that 'since an accident in Bosnia, Siân's dreams had treated her pretty roughly' (HNNS 2), hinting at PTSD, though this particular dream is somehow connected to Whitby. Early on, Siân has a chance meeting with a runner, which sets up the story's central drama. Mack is first glimpsed out running with his dog Hadrian, for whom Siân feels an immediate affection. Over the coming days, Siân and Mack talk, flirt, keep meeting on the steps or close to them. There are several confused misunderstandings, also mutual physical attraction. In urging her to run up the steps with him, for example, Mack is mortified when he discovers Siân is an amputee. He never learns she thinks she is dying from cancer (later in the story, readers discover she doesn't have cancer after all),[5] though readers see how her failing health haunts her. The story is mostly focalized through Siân; readers witness her internal tortures and suicidal fantasies, though perspective occasionally shifts momentarily to Hadrian. This is a clue as to how the story will end, also a reminder of how Faber consistently presents the non-human world – not secondary, rather another valuable perspective on events no creature fully controls or understands. Meanwhile, Siân's quiet suffering applies pressure to the plot. Her limited time impacts the decisions she makes: 'nothing dies painlessly,' she thinks. 'Even a limb that's long gone keeps hurting' (HNNS 66). A recurring motif is her *want*. She cannot have what she wants (Mack, good health, sound sleep), but wants it nonetheless. '*I want, I want, I want*' (HNNS 48), she scolds herself, feeling foolish for wanting anything at all.

Siân and Mack are brought closer together by a found text, an apparent murder confession by an 18th-century Whitby whaler turned oil merchant called Thomas Peirson, the start of which Mack can make out in a scroll. Siân, who has seen first-hand how hard it is to extract the past into the present, is morally conflicted about uncovering this confession at all. But she relents, painstakingly eking Peirson's message out of the antique bottle herself nightly, sharing what she finds with Mack during their meetings. Peirson seems to have strangled his daughter, circumstance and motivation remaining unclear.

Siân and Mack bicker during this piecemeal uncovering, having contrasting views of the past being explored in Whitby, at the Abbey, the dig too. Siân is unsettled by Mack's presence; she fears his hands as she fears her dreams, though that fear remains somehow tethered in her mind to desire. But Siân and Mack are at least united in wanting to get to the end of Peirson's confession. In one scene, they find the dead man's gravestone, another way the past inserts itself into Whitby's present. Alone one night, drunk, Siân attacks the gravestone, forgetting what she sensed from the start. Fragments of the past are, by definition, incomplete. They are often misleading. Assumptions are unwise.

Eventually, Siân discovers Peirson did not murder his daughter. Rather, he found her dead by suicide, covering up the truth to rescue her from religious disgrace. In the confession, Peirson describes spending the rest of his life tortured by this act, burying himself in Christian texts, hoping to find evidence his daughter might be spared the hellfire he believes in. Mack experiences this revelation as a different kind of horror, unable to understand what faith can lead people to do in the name of so-called respectability. Mack lives for pleasure and despises those who deny themselves. But Siân admires Peirson, also Saint Hilda, a key character in the history of the Abbey who she keeps returning to in her imagination. She reveres those who deny themselves in the name of a greater moral or religious cause. Siân and Mack are ill-suited.

Once Peirson's true confession is clear, they have little excuse to keep seeing each other. Mack has been in Whitby temporarily, putting his affairs in order after his father's death before returning home to London. At the story's end he tells Siân he must leave, their relationship left unconsummated – although their shared experience finds a surprising, lasting result. Mack gives Siân his dog Hadrian, an inheritance from his father – Siân clearly desires the pet more than Mack himself. In an emotional final scene, she is transformed as she stands on Whitby's steps once more, reaches the Abbey, then spins until delirious. Siân lies on the ground, looking up:

> With the land and sky revolving before her eyes, she laid herself down in the stone hollow, settling her shoulders and head in the proper place. For what seemed like ages, the turrets and piers of the abbey moved to and fro on the roof of the East Cliff like giant sailing ships made of rock, then finally glided to a standstill. Up there on the buttresses, the ghostie woman not only failed to jump, but failed to appear. (HNNS 136)

Here, Siân's mind is finally in her 'proper place'. She is still alive, seemingly more alive than ever. In rejecting suicide, she embraces the dizziness of her reality instead. What brings her out of her reverie in the story's final lines is Hadrian, licking her face. This animal who has become central to her story is given the last audible word:

> 'I think I'll call you Hush,' she said, elbowing herself up a little.
>
> 'Hush,' he agreed, nudging her to get to her feet. (HNNS 136)

After Siân's struggles with Mack throughout, *The Hundred and Ninety-Nine Steps* ends with this more satisfying connection, human and animal seeming to share a language in which verbal communication is secondary. Siân and Hush are made a new pair, the dog encouraging his new owner to keep going, despite it all. This has been coming since they met.

From the start, both Mack and Hadrian are connected to the steps of the title. This reminds readers the story is rooted in the conversation between past and present, but the steps also play a functional role too, bringing Siân, Mack and Hadrian together. Indeed, when Siân first spots them at the start of the story, they are heading towards the steps, Hadrian being more the focus of her attention than his owner:

> She turned. The handsome young man was sprinting up the hundred and ninety-nine steps, as easily as if he were on flat ground. His dog was bounding ahead, narrowing the distance to Siân two steps at a time. For an instant Siân felt a primeval fear at the approach of a powerful fanged creature, then relaxed as the dog scudded to a halt and sat to attention in front of her, just like a dog on a cheesy greeting card.
>
> 'He won't hurt you!' said the man, catching up, panting a little himself now. (HNNS 12)

Clearly, fear will be ever-present in this story, mixed up as it is with desire. Hadrian is the reason Mack and Siân start talking in the first place, and he often remains their focus through the interaction that follows. In that first meeting it is Hadrian to whom Siân shows immediate, uncomplicated affection. Human interaction is harder to enjoy. This is reinforced when Siân and

Mack are struggling to know how to act, what to say. They interact through Hadrian, his behaviour often described as a human's might be. When that final 'Hush' comes, it reads like this is what the story has been leading to. It all contributes to a sense that Hadrian, or Hush, is given an equal role in this story, human characters merely one part of a whole that contains the animal, the environment, the past and present too. As such, *The Hundred and Ninety-Nine Steps* is more of a recognizable Michel Faber work than it might first appear. It also helped to further solidify his reputation, further positive reviews in the likes of the *Times*, *Scotsman* and *Guardian* complemented by the fact that sales exceeded Canongate's expectations.

## *THE COURAGE CONSORT*

Like *The Hundred and Ninety-Nine Steps*, *The Courage Consort* began as a short story that kept growing, though this time no one asked for it. Originally drafted in the 1990s as a kind of 'safety valve' when his head was all too full of *The Crimson Petal*'s hugeness[6] (another commonality with *The Hundred and Ninety-Nine Steps*), the inspiration for the Consort itself came from an Australian radio interview in 1992 with Terry Edwards of the Electric Phoenix a cappella ensemble: 'I always wanted to write a story about them, but it took me a long time before I had the right feeling to put at the heart of it.'[7] The author started out not with a narrative plan or character, rather a desire to elicit a particular emotion, though by now he was aware of his own tics as a writer and was actively trying to work against these:

> By the time I wrote *The Courage Consort*, I was becoming increasingly mindful of aspects of my art which might turn into tics or 'business as usual'. I absolutely didn't want to turn into a novelist to whom the loyal fan could turn for a predictable dose of the thing they liked... I wanted to produce a radically different book each time.[8]

With this in mind, he gave Eva thumbnail sketches for characters before starting the book, asking her for traits he wouldn't have thought of himself. 'Angela' became 'Dagmar', the fiercely independent new mother who brings her baby to rehearsals. Decisions about setting, world, sound and the avant-garde followed, the language of the book and its dominant concerns being Faber's own.

He started sending out *The Courage Consort* in early 1999. Two weeks after David Jackson Young's adaptation of 'Taking Care of Big Brother' was broadcast on BBC Radio Scotland, he sent the producer *The Courage Consort*, and a version was passed around. But nothing came of this or other submissions, and it was not published until after *Under the Skin* and *The Hundred and Ninety-Nine Steps*, though it was written before both. Again, Canongate wanted more from the author. Again they asked: did he have anything else? Judy Moir preferred *The Courage Consort* to *The Hundred and Ninety-Nine Steps*. Once again, Faber was slated quickly for publication.

The critical response to *The Courage Consort* was again extremely positive, and once again the book exceeded commercial expectations, which were modest for a 'novella' – though this book was crowded out by Faber's others. *The Hundred and Ninety-Nine Steps* had been published just seven months before, in July 2001; the paperback of *Under the Skin* was also published in that year, and *The Crimson Petal* was published just eight months after *The Courage Consort*, in October 2002. *The Courage Consort* is a quieter work, standing in stark contrast to *The Crimson Petal* in particular. That was a kind of rebuke to the traditional Victorian historical novel, revelling in its directness and visceral nature, whereas *The Courage Consort* is understated throughout, subtle in its character portraits. It presents a world that may seem rarefied to some readers. *The Crimson Petal* was also published in many more countries and languages, giving it a broader reach.

In its first UK edition, *The Courage Consort* received favourable reviews in the literary pages of, among others, the *Daily Telegraph*, *Daily Mail*, *Scotsman* and *Guardian*. Some concentrated partially on the book itself and partially on the nature and value of Faber's fast-growing body of work, also his place in the Scottish literary landscape. Canongate catalogues foregrounded review quotes putting him alongside major contemporary Scottish writers like Ali Smith, James Kelman, A.L. Kennedy and Alasdair Gray. *The Courage Consort* was Faber's fourth book in five years, with the most highly anticipated of all coming. (The *Guardian* review even mentioned the as-yet-unpublished *Crimson Petal* by name.)

Understandably, *The Courage Consort* was somewhat sidelined. It deserves to be assessed outside of its initial context.

Commonalities between *The Hundred and Ninety-Nine Steps* and *The Courage Consort* have often been noted. Aside from being written in a similar period, and growing out of short stories, there are more meaningful connections. In each book, the female protagonists, Siân and Catherine, mediate the narrative for readers, moving between internal monologue and external drama. In each book, these women consider suicide. Siân thinks she is dying; Catherine does not know how to live. Each story is a study in haunting. As Faber told the *Barcelona Review*: 'I wanted to convey how it feels to have been depressed and numb for a long time, and to come back to life. Catherine is like a soul waking up from anaesthesia. That's scary, but inspiring too.'[9] That description might also apply to Siân.

In some editions these two medium-sized stories have been published in the same volume. For instance, readers ordering a copy of the 2010 UK paperback of *The Hundred and Ninety-Nine Steps* might have been surprised to find *The Courage Consort* hiding inside it. The fact that the former is very much the headline act, the latter relegated to a barely visible mention on the book jacket's reverse, suggests one was considered more commercial than the other, though in 2004 *The Courage Consort* was given lead billing in that 'three novellas' edition, where once again the two stories were tied together.

*The Courage Consort* is the story of a semi-famous a cappella vocal ensemble who spend an intense fortnight preparing for their latest commissioned performance in a Belgian chateau deep in a forest with a wartime Nazi past, from which the forest itself seems to be recovering. The piece the ensemble are tackling is the complicated, possibly unperformable *Partitum Mutante*. Notable partly for its focus on avant-garde music, a lifelong preoccupation of the author (by now he had been contemplating some kind of non-fiction book on the subject for over 20 years), and partly for being a rare Faber book to feature actual Dutch characters (though minor, they are there – even Dutch bikes feature), this work focuses on the mental distress of, and sexual tensions between, members of The Courage Consort. This ensemble is led by the serious, determined Roger Courage. His wife Catherine is lead soprano, with tenor Julian Hind,

German mountain-climber Dagmar Belotte (and her newborn baby) along with the physically imposing bass Benjamin Lamb making up the rest of the cast sketched out by Eva. They make for a compellingly dysfunctional choral family, one seen thrown into mundane proximity to each other for longer than they are used to, two weeks' preparation time in relative luxury being rare for them. Rehearsals are disrupted by the composer's whims as well as by a recurring mysterious cry from the woods, this being another Faber work where the characters seem to be in an ongoing wrestling match with their environment.

In 2002, reviews noted Catherine Courage was just the latest of Faber's 'heroine[s]' on the verge of a nervous breakdown'. Her mental state is immediately clear:

> On the day the good news arrived, Catherine spent her first few waking hours toying with the idea of jumping out the window of her apartment. Toying was perhaps too mild a word; she actually opened the window and sat on the sill, wondering if four storeys was enough to make death certain. She didn't fancy the prospect of quadriplegia, as she hated hospitals, with their peculiar synthesis of fuss and boredom. Straight to the grave was best. If she could only drop from a height of a thousand storeys into soft, spongey ground, maybe her body would even bury itself on impact. (TCC 1)

This opening is suggestive of the author's employed tone throughout. Oddly comic and strangely understated, Catherine is shown to be contemplating suicide in a vague, distracted way, the extent of her urge to disappear largely hidden from her husband. Roger and Catherine's relationship is one of *The Courage Consort*'s most convincing elements. Neither seeks to hurt the other, though Roger's ego is bruised by Catherine's repeated rejection of his advances, while she fears sex with him, seeing him as an oppressor she is trapped alongside in bed. Catherine has been dependent all her life, first on her father, then on Roger; her fortnight in Belgium eventually suggests what independence might look like. But until then, outside the bedroom at least, she is managed by Roger at every turn. En route to the chateau, Catherine reflects that 'she almost always felt much younger than other people, unless they were clearly minors. This wasn't vanity on her part; it was inferiority. Everyone had negotiated their passage into adulthood except her. She was still waiting to be called' (TCC 11).

This passivity is her defining feature, though the longer the group spends in the chateau, the more readers see, through her various outbursts (so embarrassing to Roger), how others perceive her. Also, readers learn where that passivity comes from. She has an extraordinary voice but Catherine lives without confidence, without making decisions for herself. In one scene she reveals, as if mentioning what she had for breakfast, that her mother, a cellist in the BBC Symphony Orchestra, committed suicide when Catherine was a young girl. Catherine reports to the group that she found her mother with a UNICEF polythene bag over her head, one 'with pictures of smiling children all over it'.

No wonder Catherine has lived as if frozen ever since. Even her relationship with sound is immobile; she sings *Partitum Mutante* as instructed to, without a thought for her own instincts – which makes any meaningful connection, that most enduring of Faber concerns, as impossible as the repair of her marriage. But, through her developing relationship with the pragmatic Dagmar, with whom she goes cycling, and Ben, for whom she enjoys making *havermout* in the mornings, it becomes clear: Catherine *is* capable of contentment. When the group breaks out into a long argument about whether or not to perform *Partitum Mutante*, Catherine retreats. She has begun to feel more youthful in recent days, more confident, independent too. In the midst of the fighting she looks at Ben, for whom she has genuine affection, and considers an act of treachery, thinking: *'Dare I do something that might lead to the end of two marriages?'* (TCC 132). Like Siân in *The Hundred and Ninety-Nine Steps*, she is unrecognizable as the woman readers met on the first page. Like Siân, she fantasizes about potentially destructive behaviour as a way to break out of the unstated impasse of her circumstances.

As Justine Jordan, now Deputy Literary Editor of the *Guardian*, identified in a glowing review, documenting the lives of women adrift was already a familiar trope of Faber's work – and here was another, different kind. Jordan also saw this book in the context of Faber's previous one, though she preferred *The Courage Consort*. In Jordan's view, *The Hundred and Ninety-Nine Steps* was a 'short story suffering from overwork', whereas *The Courage Consort* was 'a considered and delicately achieved whole', steering away from the outlandishness of previous works like *Under the*

*Skin* to 'map a more recognisable territory of psychological hurt'. The map of the book places the chateau in conversation with the apparently haunted landscape around it, also with music itself – confusing, terrifying, impossible to navigate, impossible to understand. Each of these elements plays a crucial role in the slowly unfurling narrative, delivered, as Jordan writes, 'in scrupulously unobtrusive prose', Faber drawing characters 'with assured comic efficiency while conjuring Catherine's hypersensitive consciousness, the oppressive weight of the world and "acoustic immensity" of the forest outside'. The contrast between the immensity of the natural world around them and the smallness of the Consort's domestic circumstance makes for a potent mix. This was noted by Jamie Jauncey in *The Scotsman*, who pointed to what unites the author's many disparate works:

> [T]he most striking aspect of the book, and the one which perhaps most characterises Faber's writing, is his honesty and compassion. He is fiercely inventive, his plotting is wholly unpredictable, but he pulls no tricks. Where his characters experience transformation, and not all of them do, they do so with great subtlety.[10]

*The Courage Consort* contains a surprising, highly charged ending. The weather finally breaks in Belgium, arguments between the group cease, rain finally comes and Benjamin Lamb lies prostrate on the chateau floor, Dagmar and Catherine trying to breathe life back into him. They fail. Eventually Roger, ever the professional, broaches the impossible subject – will they go on? Finally an adult like the others, Catherine can respond. For what may be the first time, she tells Roger *no*. She informs a caller that of course The Courage Consort will not be performing *Partitum Mutante* at the Benelux Music Festival; they are in mourning. Catherine makes the decision for everyone. On the bus on the way back to the airport, she acts once more, now determined not to forever anguish but to 'get on with it', 'it' being her life: 'Instinctively, to fill the void, Catherine began to sing: the simplest, most comforting little song she knew... The terrible silence was receding, that was the main thing' (TCC 144). Soon, the others join in with her. It is almost a happy ending.

## THE FAHRENHEIT TWINS

This is a medium-sized story with a long history. It was drafted fast, in July and August of 1998, when Faber was at an advanced stage of editorial with *Some Rain Must Fall*. He suggested including it but was discouraged. He remembers:

> Jamie wasn't keen on it. I don't think he 'got' it. Rather than trying to persuade him to see the story as I saw it, I was just delighted that he was enthusiastic about so many of my other stories. There were clearly too many to fit into one collection so some had to be excluded in any case. Excluding one because my publisher didn't like it seemed an excellent reason.[11]

Seen in isolation it might seem curious that 'The Fahrenheit Twins' was not noticed, it now being widely regarded as one of Faber's standout works. But as his database shows, this was just one of a clutch of new stories he was working on through 1998, some of which were never published at all.

One of these was 'Adopt a Tiger', which was submitted widely before eventually being published in *Big Issue Australia*. Within weeks of writing 'The Fahrenheit Twins', another new story, called 'Bed & Breakfast', was abandoned. (Later finished, that was eventually published too, in *The Erotic Review*.) 'Me and My First Wife' (later re-titled 'Hole'), written in the September of 1998, was never published. In November 1998 he re-wrote the old story 'The Broccoli Eel', submitting it to several competitions and BBC Radio Scotland, without success. (This story was eventually published by *The Guardian* in 2003, after the success of *The Crimson Petal*, when demand for his fiction was at its height.) None of these made the cut for either of Faber's own short-story collections. Looking back now, 'The Fahrenheit Twins' seems like an anomaly in an otherwise fallow period for Faber's short fiction – this when the *Some Rain Must Fall* manuscript was already too big. Soon after, attention returned to novel-writing anyway. In 1999, he concentrated on *Under the Skin* and *The Crimson Petal*. He did submit 'The Fahrenheit Twins' and an early, longer version of 'The Safehouse' to Kevin Williamson of Rebel Inc. for the *Last Exit to Leith* anthology, though that book was never published.[12] Too long for most anthologies or competitions, too short to be a novel, and already rejected by his UK publisher, it looked like 'The Fahrenheit Twins' might be forgotten.

Indirectly, it was rescued by the success of *The Crimson Petal*, which led to increased interest in the US. American publisher Harcourt suggested a volume of novellas. The author offered *The Hundred and Ninety-Nine Steps* and *The Courage Consort*, but the publisher wanted a fatter book. At this point, there was still no home for this medium-sized story with its uncommon character names, hard-to-define genre blend, uncommon setting and length that seemed to please no one. So in 2004 'The Fahrenheit Twins' was published as one novella of three by Harcourt in the US. The *Three Novellas* volume sold poorly, and that year Judy Moir left Canongate for Penguin, but Jamie Byng revisited the story afresh shortly after, when working with Faber on selections for his second UK collection. When that book was published, 'The Fahrenheit Twins' was, along with 'The Safehouse', the story which garnered the most positive response. An image of the twins' respective shadows, facing in opposite directions in front of an all-white Arctic background, made for a jacket which very much foregrounded the story's centrality – and it gave its name to the collection.

In 2009, the reputation of 'The Fahrenheit Twins' grew further when it was adapted into a play staged at the Barbican, London, produced by the experimental theatre company Told By an Idiot. This toured widely, to considerable acclaim. Since then, 'The Fahrenheit Twins' has had a wider cultural impact. The story was made into a podcast with music by Brian Eno.[13] A Dutch multi-instrumentalist duo, Sander Blom and Teun Duijghuisen, even named their band after the story.[14] This strange genesis is an example of how the seemingly random, sometimes contradictory demands of the publishing industry, also questions of timing and luck, can impact how a story is received, where it is published or if it is published at all.

'The Fahrenheit Twins' is the story of a pair of boy-and-girl twins called Tainto'lilith and Marko'cain. They are raised in the Arctic, on an island exploration station called Ostrov Providenya with their German anthropologist parents, Boris and Una. As Sue Zlosnik, professor of Gothic Literature at Manchester Metropolitan University, notes, Faber sets the story 'where Mary Shelley left *Frankenstein*, in the frozen wastes of the

Arctic'. Situating it firmly in the Gothic tradition, she describes 'The Fahrenheit Twins' as a 'tale of a quest for origin and anxiety about destination. Its twenty-first century wilderness provides the setting for a mythopoeic tale about the moribund nature of Western culture.'[15]

In her essay on this story, 'Globalgothic at the Top of the World', Zlosnik argues that 'much of [Faber's] writing succeeds in sustaining a sense of the uncanny'.[16] That seems particularly evident in this story of 'a latter-day Hansel and Gretel'. The children are between seven and eleven years old; no one recorded their date of birth. The twins do not look like either of their parents. They both have exactly the same 'scattering of tiny puckered scars' (TFT 233), relics of an illness that threatened their survival, then disappeared. Boris and Una, meanwhile, are very much of 'the Old World' – Europe, that is, a place whose everyday items (cuckoo clocks, for example) take on an uncanny power when transplanted, as if from space, into the Arctic landscape.

Una and Boris are world-leading scholars who study the local indigenous Guhiynui population, though they are somewhat less interested in their own children. This makes this family unit of four sometimes read more like a pair, though the twins are invariably accompanied by their 'team of huskies'. (Again, animals are an important part of a Faber narrative. Faber writes of the twins, 'They conversed with the huskies as equals' (TFT 233).) Like Faber's other medium-sized stories assessed in this chapter, 'The Fahrenheit Twins' has a small cast: father, mother, twins and huskies. It has a singular narrative focus, with no secondary plot strands or diversions. Also, it is set in this one striking geographical location, with the Arctic described in all its brilliance and vividity, as haunting a backdrop as the steps of Whitby or the dark forests of Belgium.

That haunting is present in the landscape from the start, though it is described as heavenly: 'At the icy zenith of the world, far away from any other children, Tainto'lilith and Marko'cain knew no better than that life was bliss. Therefore, it *was* bliss' (TFT 231). The italicization of the word 'was' displays how Faber's apparently plain prose style can obscure a subtextual charge. Tainto'lilith and Marko'cain (each name a part-echo of the Biblical Lilith and Cain) realize they have been missing something essential.

There may be no limit to the time they can play, in this place of 'almost-perpetual Arctic twilight' (TFT 231). Faber writes, 'The Fahrenheits were monarchs here, and their two children prince and princess' (TFT 232). There may be no borders in their world, no territory out of bounds. But that opening passage suggests their bliss is an illusion, about to be shattered.

Tainto'lilith and Marko'cain have free rein in what seems an impossibly large garden, where they can play, learn essential skills for survival and develop their own rituals as they please. In this icy Garden of Eden, the children write their own pseudo-bible, made up of occasional things their mother says about the world. (She hardly ever addresses them; when she does, they take notice.) Tainto'lilith and Marko'cain record these statements with earnest reverence, then return to their record for guidance in times of need. They call this text the Book of Knowledge (a nod to the Tree of Knowledge, from which Adam and Eve were forbidden to eat). Judeo-Christian religious echoes are evident across multiple Faber fictions, from *The Fire Gospel* to *The Book of Strange New Things*. But the biblical subtext of 'The Fahrenheit Twins' has been somewhat less commented upon. Seen through this lens, it reads like a tale of the Fall, from innocence to a burgeoning maturity, in which differences between males and females, and the 'God' they worship, have tragic and irreversible consequences.

Like most of Faber's narratives, 'The Fahrenheit Twins' is told in third person, close up. The main difference here is that the narrative is delivered from close to *two* characters. This fractures later on, when the pressures of their situation lead them to see themselves and each other differently – but at the story's outset, Tainto'lilith and Marko'cain are presented as one. For a writer who has repeatedly returned to stories where genuine human understanding is elusive, it is interesting to observe Faber's preoccupations at work in a story where the two central characters are genetically and physically almost identical. The first time they speak, they speak together:

'What lies beyond?' the twins once asked their father.

'Nothing special,' Boris Fahrenheit replied without looking up from his journals.

'What lies beyond?' they then asked their mother, knowing she tended to see things rather differently. (TFT 232)

No distinction is made between Tainto'lilith and Marko'cain here, no hint given as to the voice of each child – who is louder, who starts or finishes speaking first. The lines are written as if the twins are one. This is made explicit, their similarity presented as magical:

> The indistinguishable cots [their father built] were apt. In all respects except genitals, Tainto'lilith and Marko'cain were identical twins. Their expressions were the same. There was even the same amount of light inside their eyes, a difficult thing to reproduce. (TFT 234)

Their sense of being essentially the same is disrupted when Una tells her children a story – that in the future 'their bodies would change beyond recognition' (TFT 234). The twins laugh, with one voice. This serves to establish them as supernaturally connected, two child-gods in a story which undoubtedly has fantasy genre elements. (There is something of the secondary world fantasy sub-genre about both setting and tonal delivery, though Ostrov Provideniya – spelled slightly differently – is a little-known part of Earth.)

Even as their mother's story causes them anxiety, it does so in a way that appears to reinforce the twins' indivisibility. A reader familiar with Faber's methods and preoccupations might, at this stage, begin to wonder if they're reading an exception in the oeuvre – a story where two people genuinely understand each other, in totality. But then their unity starts to fracture, fearful as they are that somehow they will be pulled apart by biology. Amid this fear, they finally speak individually. At this point in the narrative, they have just imagined how they might resist the changing of the seasons, doing so by enacting a ritual they have just made up, which involves an eternally reincarnated fox getting its eyes stabbed out.

> 'Do you think it will work?' asked Tainto'lilith.
>
> 'I'm sure of it,' Marko'cain assured her. 'I feel it in my testaments.'
>
> Having said that, there could be no doubt. (TFT 236)

Marko'cain is wrong, of course – nothing can stop the changing of the seasons. And the more he senses the future in 'his testaments' (TFT 236) (or 'testicles' – this is, after all, the only evident biological difference between them so far), the more vulnerable the twins will become.

The story's opening establishes, in reflective passages examining the twins' early lives, that '[m]ore than anything, the twins' characters were formed by benign neglect' (TFT 233). (The story is written as if out of time: note the phrase 'the twins once asked their father' in the above quote, with no date given, no story timeline established.) Distance is suggested between the parents, whose Old World intrudes on their present, and the children, who only know their current world. This reads as an echo of the relationship between Janet and Kif Kif in 'Fish'; the Old World touching the present through the memories of Boris and Una is reminiscent, too, of *The Hundred and Ninety-Nine Steps*. Faber's familiar preoccupations are present here, written into a different context. Boundaries *do* exist in this place, between the Fahrenheits and the off-stage Guhiynui people, also between the parents and their children, and potentially between the children themselves. The twins' parents visit the Guhiynui regularly, leaving Tainto'lilith and Marko'cain alone. The only rule is that they must never leave home without a compass, as the icy tundra, untouched as it is, makes it hard to distinguish north from south, east from west. The compass will soon become a symbol of how lost they truly are.

The story's turning point is the sudden death of Una Fahrenheit. The twins are left confused and distraught, not least by the response of their distant father. He does not care what happens to his wife's body, leaving the decision as to what to do with it with the twins. After considerable anguishing, they seek an appropriate ritual for this momentous tragedy, embarking on a solemn journey with their huskies to lay Una to rest in the appropriate place, wherever that might be. As they soon discover, Boris acts as spoiler here, pretending with apparent, uncharacteristic, enthusiasm to make sure that the twins have all they need for their journey, while doing his best to ensure they don't survive the trip. He pretends to fill their rucksack with food. (They later discover, far from home, that he has filled it with balls of paper and a copy of the *Principia Anthropologica*, which they must burn for warmth.) The huskies nearly die of hunger. The compass breaks (or was purposely broken). Then, miraculously, the twins stumble upon a Guhiynui tribe hut which is a shrine to Una, replete with German cuckoo clocks, a bed of seal skins, also 'a dynamic full-length portrait of a dark-skinned male and a slender creamy-white female... meant to be Una Fahrenheit' (TFT 267). The twins do not realize this may be the place of their own origin – that perhaps their father is the Guhiynui man in the portrait with their mother – though they do know their mother is revered here, and take this as a sign from the universe. Briefly, the children are intuitively connected once more:

> Without needing to confer on the decision, the twins helped each other unbuckle their mother's body from the sledge and carry her into the Guhiynui house. Reverently they inserted her into the bed, wrapping the seal skins around her, smoothing her penumbra of wet hair evenly over the pillow. (TFT 269)

Finally, they have found their ritual. They sleep on the sledge as the huskies pull them homeward. They arrive half-dead, though they will survive this ordeal. Another one awaits them at the door to the Fahrenheit family home.

As an act of betrayal, the moment of Boris's paralysis at the twins' return is one of the most shocking passages in Faber's oeuvre – in language suggestive of an act of God, he is described as being 'thunderstruck'. Boris assumed the landscape would claim them; he is already busy living his new life, free, he believes, of fatherhood, when Tainto'lilith and Marko'cain walk into the family home. Though Boris's plan is heavily trailed (on the tundra, the children speculate over whether Boris tried to kill them), readers soon receive a new shock. The twins find their mother has been replaced by one Miss Kristensen. She is already used to living in the house, having no idea Boris was a father. One reason 'The Fahrenheit Twins' bears repeated readings is because Boris's motivation is never explained, nor his new relationship fully explored. Nor do readers discover whether the twins' father orchestrated their mother's death.

On this day of their return, Tainto'lilith and Marko'cain lock themselves in the bathroom, stunned, unsure how to respond. Their new reality is undeniable, their differences too, with

Tainto'lilith horrified by Marko'cain's attitude to the prospect of murdering their father, even to murdering Miss Kristensen, this new Old World presence who seems delighted to discover they exist. The story ends with Marko'cain glibly suggesting various ways they could escape their Arctic world for 'a green place' (TFT 276). At this point, Faber brings the twins closer together for a moment, but only to illustrate their unbridgeable distance. On the story's final page, Tainto'lilith is crying:

> Marko'cain, catching sight of her distress, was shocked. She had never wept without him before, particularly not in a situation where he himself could imagine nothing to weep about. Awkwardly, he patted her trembling shoulders. Now he too glimpsed a lifetime ahead of him, of trying, and failing, to comfort his sister in her secret sorrows. (TFT 276)

Tainto'lilith and Marko'cain get closer to true connection, perhaps, than any two characters in Michel Faber's fiction. And yet, by the story's dread-filled ending, they find themselves not only apart, but unable to see how that separation can ever be undone.

Dread is central to 'The Fahrenheit Twins', which partly explains its power. As Nicholas Prescott has it in his essay 'Echoes of Poe: Absence and the Uncanny in "The Fahrenheit Twins" and *The Courage Consort*', there is a 'compelling and curious kind of dread... operating centrally' in 'The Fahrenheit Twins', something he compares to the stories of Edgar Allen Poe (MFCE 97). This tale certainly has a creeping, Poe-like horror at its heart which feels inevitable from that opening italicised '*was*'. It explores the terrible fractures that can happen in the 'little paradise' of the happy nuclear family in a piece where, once more for Faber, an unforgiving natural landscape acts as a backdrop for a drama in which true closeness is, if not completely an illusion, then certainly a fleeting thing.

# 3

# Faber's World of the Novel

## INTRODUCTION

So far, chapters in this book have addressed Michel Faber as a writer of short and 'medium-sized' stories. This one traces his development in the longer form via three case studies – two highly celebrated books and one unpublished manuscript. Each finds Faber in a different stage of his writing life, practising compassionate approaches in the novel form over a period of 30 years. The first case study, *A Photograph of Jesus*, represents the early stage. This novel was seen by hardly anyone except the author's first wife until now, being discarded before Faber met Eva Youren.[1] The second, *Under the Skin*, represents Faber's middle period, a study in compassion seen through the consequences of its absence. *The Book of Strange New Things* represents late-era Faber, the writer's 'last novel for adults' being a 'goodbye book' written while Eva was slowly dying from cancer.

*Under the Skin* and *The Book of Strange New Things* are sometimes discussed together as being Faber's two 'science fiction' novels. Neither can be easily categorized, but they do have commonalities. Both are highly conceptual in nature, interplanetary in setting, and both feature invented language. They have significant differences too, though. *The Book of Strange New Things* is a book about enduring love, while *Under the Skin* features a protagonist with little experience of even the most temporary kind. Meanwhile, the latter represents Faber's most successful attempt at something he had been trying to achieve for 30 years. This effort persisted through multiple fictions as diverse in size and nature as *The Fire Gospel*, *The Crimson Petal* and stories like 'The Fahrenheit Twins'. In all these works and more, Faber sought to construct a 'compassionate and genuinely enquiring' study of faith where readers would be encouraged to resist having a 'superior attitude' to religious characters.[2] This chapter begins with the author's first sustained attempt at that task, and ends with arguably his most successful.

## EARLY WORKS AND *A PHOTOGRAPH OF JESUS*

Michel Faber has been a novelist since he was a teenager, though he destroyed almost all the evidence of this when he was in his mid-twenties.[3] Predictably, some of these works were derivative, though from early on Faber had an instinct for realizing characters with a rich inner life, and also had an evident talent for conceptual thinking. Certainly, he was good enough to publish by the mid-1980s. And yet he wrote for 20 years in total without trying to.

Critics have sometimes responded with wonder to the fact that any artist could exist for so long in isolation, creating so much then repeatedly discarding their work in this way, without seeking validation from the outside world. It is unusual. But Faber was practising, in private, while growing in confidence. In the 80s there was the benefit of relative financial security; he had no dependents, few expenses, and his nursing job meant he did not need to make money from fiction yet. In 1987, having recently finished a draft of *The Crimson Petal*, he started a new, contemporary novel called *A Photograph of Jesus*. Once it was complete, the writer set it aside in early 1988, only briefly returning to the manuscript a year or two later to tinker with marginal details.

Set in St Kilda, Melbourne, *A Photograph of Jesus* tells the story of Martin Brophy, a computer programmer in the late pre-internet age who is about to receive a 'positive identification as Jesus Christ' (POJ 1). At the novel's outset, Martin's non-work life largely revolves around obsessively videotaping TV programmes across two machines, while recording LPs for selling on. From Frankie Goes to Hollywood pin-up books to Foreigner on the radio, the novel is soaked in pop culture. Brand names, shops, TV programmes and albums are all capitalized in the old Word Perfect document the novel was written on, suggesting a commonality between these elements in Faber's Aussie, suburban, consumerist void. Four years before *American Psycho*, the zeitgeist-capturing novel by Brett Easton Ellis, a writer Faber disliked for his lack of compassion (he once wrote to Canongate explicitly asking them not to send the author a copy of *The Crimson Petal*), Faber was busy writing a very different kind of highly dysfunctional male. Also 'full of hatred' (POJ 73), also living an empty life, also all-too-attached to his record collection, the approaches used to present that void by Faber and Easton Ellis respectively were nevertheless opposed. Reading this novel now, surface-level commonalities are obvious. But where Ellis provides overstatement, the horror of self-obsession and the shock of slaughter, Faber's every instinct is to understate, using the same consumerist society as a way to explore sensitivity, belief and faith.

Martin lives alone, but *A Photograph of Jesus* is a family story. Martin's sister Alannah is the presenter of premier Australian news show *As It Happens*. He mostly interacts with her through the TV screen, scrolling back and forth through her reports, looking for a particular expression on her face. The Brophys, as Martin puts it, have 'failed validity tests' over and over (POJ 56). Father Len, who prefers Alannah to Martin to an embarrassing degree, is dying in a nursing home. (Later, the disturbing nature of his obsession is made explicit.) His mother left the family years ago, after an affair. She spends her retirement playing bowls on the Gold Coast, oddly disconnected. Martin avoids them all.

Though, to his frustration, he can't edit his own life, at least Martin likes his job: for him and colleague Alex, there is 'nothing so satisfying in all the universe as making computers do stuff' (POJ 19). This provides respite from an otherwise lonely routine, where Martin is liable to go down 'The Gloom Tube' of depression. Then, leaving the office one day, he is photographed by a small group called The New Wave Christians of the Seventh Seal, who believe Martin will soon 'become' Christ. First, he tries to escape the believers. Then he tries reason. But nothing can put them off: the scriptures have predicted his resistance. Soon, the New Wave Christians move into the flat above his, keeping an eye on their messiah. Martin becomes the centre of a media storm.

In discussions with the author about this novel, sent to me as part of the process for this book, Faber described *A Photograph of Jesus* as being a precursor to *The Book of Strange New Things*. Initially, I associated the two so closely that I approached this novel looking for evidence of what it would become many years later. This gave way to confusion. On first reading, *A Photograph of Jesus* seemed to me, if anything, a version of *The Fire Gospel*, in which a similarly slobby, obsessive–compulsive and vaguely sexist single man finds himself becoming famous overnight. But the real connection between *A Photograph of Jesus* and *The Book of Strange New Things* is the exploration of faith. Yes, these novels are set in different countries, different time periods and mostly on different planets. The narrative threads have little in common. But for the author, they represent two attempts at the same thing.

*A Photograph of Jesus* is a coherent and complete novel, with fully fleshed-out characters and an engaging story, but Faber soon decided there were two main things wrong with it. The first related to Martin himself, a protagonist he considered to be of a clearly identifiable, already-outdated type:

> My low opinion of the book is not because I think it was poorly executed. I knew what I was doing by then. But there are so many books about that kind of spiritually empty male existence, written by gloomy self-absorbed males in their thirties.[4]

I find this a little reductive, harsh too. Yes, there are many books of this type. Faber references *Withnail and I* as an example – that film (coincidentally, released in 1987) must have seemed emblematic. I can imagine why it would feel the time for such a novel had already passed. But Martin's family story, subtly rendered and affecting, as well as the genuine exploration of belief and obsession, seem to me worthwhile assets of a novel that, 35 years after composition, still reads well.

For Faber, the second thing wrong with *A Photograph of Jesus* was the portrayal of the New Wave Christians and their relationship with their messiah. On a sentence-to-sentence level it was fine, but Faber believed he had failed at the most important task of the project: rendering the sect and their alleged messiah with sufficient sensitivity to make readers take them seriously. The New Wave Christians arguably read like comic characters, who readers might laugh *at*. In our email exchanges Faber explained his intentions: 'the cult who latch onto Martin are supposed to be lost souls in need of comfort but I bet that for most readers they would just be tragicomic losers like the kidnappers in *The Fire Gospel*'.[5] This was not something that could be corrected with tweaks. The fundamentals of the narrative – from the seemingly random selection of Martin as unlikely messiah, to the sect hovering at his window, watching him in his kitchen, to the fact they literally follow him around Melbourne – all this was too absurdly satirical to be genuinely enquiring. It was another good run at novel-writing, but not one Faber could use. For him, the project was dead.

Though the author is adamant he will never return to this work, I believe future Faber scholars will find *A Photograph of Jesus* interesting, not least because it acts as an intriguing precursor to later novels. Peppered throughout Martin's story, concerns and approaches Faber utilized in later books are evident. For example, *A Photograph of Jesus* heavily relies on the epistolary form, which Faber would go on to use so often. Believers post letters to Martin direct, while the New Wave Christians spread word via a written leaflet explaining why Martin is marked for greatness. A letter also plays a crucial role in the novel's denouement, when believer and sort-of love interest Lizette loses her faith at the last. There is also an occasional all-seeing narrator present here that may feel familiar to readers of *The Crimson Petal*. As Faber writes, 'The last straw, or what seemed like the last straw to Martin because he couldn't read the rest of this book the way you are doing, came one afternoon after work' (POJ 84). Some of these elements are marginal, though the study of faith is substantial. As we shall see, all this was ultimately part of the journey towards the creation of Peter in *The Book of Strange New Things*.

The eternal search for connection is evident in *A Photograph of Jesus* in several ways. Martin is as alienated as any other Faber protagonist. Impossibly disconnected from his family and allergic to relationships beyond carefully limited sexual one-offs, the closest he comes to genuine connection is with technology. He keeps reaching for that, even as it denies him satisfaction. Martin is always looking for that perfect edit, perfect code. Though when his notoriety grows, he loses even that small pleasure. Sacked from his job, his home broken into, his beloved machines stolen, Martin finds connection elusive, especially with those who believe he is about to 'become Jesus'. He looks at his followers and sees only madness. Even Lizette's kindness goes unreciprocated. In his anguish, he cannot see it for what it is. And he cannot trust a believer.

Good, self-aware writers notice their early working patterns and attempt to improve these as they gain experience. Faber realized two things after *A Photograph of Jesus*. First, that on a line-to-line basis, he now knew he possessed the necessary linguistic control to tell a compelling long story. Second, he realized he had further to go in terms of thinking about what *kinds* of stories he wanted to tell and how. Development, therefore, was no longer a matter of learning how to write novels, but rather, of asking himself what kind of novelist he wanted to be. *A Photograph of Jesus* was, undoubtedly, a story of its time. He wanted to write timeless stories. His next novel would be one.

## *UNDER THE SKIN*

If all Michel Faber's fictions are, in some form, about alienation and the search for connection, *Under the Skin* may be the most powerful example of this. Published in 2000, it was described by the author as his personal 'journey from alienness [in my youth] to humanity',[6] also acting as his most ambitious exploration so far of otherness and othering. For him, *Under the Skin* was about 'the way people give themselves permission to treat other people badly... It is this notion that the other person is a different kind of life form and therefore, you can do whatever you like to them because they are not like you, they don't suffer like you, they are not important like you.'[7] In other words, he was identifying a failure in compassion. Then challenging it.

In the last 20 years, much critical analysis has been published on *Under the Skin*, a novel which David Mitchell, acclaimed author of *Cloud Atlas*, described as containing 'one of the best-orchestrated reveals in modern British fiction' (UTS vii). Isserley's story has provoked discussion around gender politics, vegetarianism, body issues, the animal, also genre hybridity in contemporary fiction. Meanwhile, the novel's broader cultural impact represents another area rich for potential exploration. These are all worthwhile entry points for a staggeringly ambitious, complex, nuanced piece of work, approachable in so many ways. Then there is the novel's alternative life as the Jonathan Glazer-directed, multi-award-winning avant-garde film starring Scarlett Johansson. Any attempt to cover this ground in a short book could only fail. Instead, I intend to do two simple things here: first, discuss the creative process, utilizing the as-yet-unseen Canongate archives. And second, summarize the narrative for new readers, seeing both these parts of the process – creation and final manuscript – through a particular lens: Faber's lifelong attempt to write effective, compassionate novels.

### The Process

*Under the Skin* underwent a transformative creative journey. Initially influenced by Faber's experiences of witnessing surgery as a nurse, and his horror at people choosing to have plastic surgery to 'look more normal',[8] it began as a story about 'a childless couple who abduct a baby monkey, shave its fur off, pay for it to be surgically modified to resemble a human, then introduce it into society as their child'. But as ever, Faber was primarily interested in developing an emotional effect, in this case changing the original concept beyond recognition to fit:

> I wanted it to be a thought-provoking tale about difference and the extent to which our culture is willing to accommodate or even tolerate it. But the more I mulled on it, the clearer it became that the novel would be a satire. I didn't want to write a satire. I wanted to write a book that knocked people sideways, haunted them for ever.[9]

Having previously discarded *A Photograph of Jesus* as a 'satire' that was not 'genuinely searching', the sheer distance this novel travelled in its early incarnations is interesting. Faber changed everything – narrative set-up, characters, world – to fit his desired emotional territory. Germinating in the mid-1990s and begun in earnest in 1997 after those short-story breakthroughs,

Faber knew his next move was important. Showing it only to Eva, he wrote and revised the manuscript extensively for nearly a year without even mentioning it to Canongate. Articles from *The Independent* magazine, still kept in the author's personal archive, show how Faber's conception of 'Isserley's original form' altered, now seeing her physically as a blend of a woman and a llama.[10]

By 1998, it had been nearly half a decade since Eva suggested her husband give up the day job. Though incremental progress had been made, with *Some Rain Must Fall* doing unusually well for a first collection, Faber was highly conscious of his financial dependence, and he remained fearful of a marginal existence. After a lifetime of rejecting his own novels, did he have the confidence and ability to carry off one as outlandish as this? *A Photograph of Jesus* was, perhaps, too safe. But was *Under the Skin* not safe enough? A particular scene gave him pause. So much so that he initially planned to simply have Isserley block out a traumatic sexual experience, rather than present it to the reader.

Early drafts show all of Chapter 9 being just a few short paragraphs, the text ending with Isserley's typically defensive insistence that 'Nothing else happened. Nothing.' In Faber's plan, this was followed by ten blank pages. Eva called this 'copping out', the blankness a 'metatextual gimmick in a novel that otherwise got by without such devices'. Initially, the two found themselves at an impasse – Faber thought he couldn't 'write more about what Isserley was going through on that jetty without becoming intrusive as an author and betraying the parameters of Isserley's voice'. But then, a breakthrough. He asked Eva to write out a version herself of how the scene might look.[11] This allowed Faber to envision it, then write it in his own words, with greater confidence. (They would return to this approach several times with later books.) All this essential collaborative work took place before the book was sent to Judy Moir in November 1998.

After being the first at the publisher to read *Under the Skin*, Moir wrote a glowing editorial report for colleagues:

> [Faber] is brilliant at making the mundane and ordinary miraculous and fresh. He can also make the extraordinary/outrageous utterly believable... I think it's a must for Canongate. It should also have

wide international appeal... Some moments of sheer poetry. Some moments that make your flesh crawl.'[12]

For Moir, part of the novel's power was its element of surprise: She remembers: 'I had no idea it would have a "sci-fi" element, so was shocked when it dawned on me why Isserley was picking up the hitchhikers.'[13] She wanted to retain that element of surprise for readers. When the time came, she would write the blurb herself, ensuring nothing was given away. Byng was as enthusiastic as Moir, and in May 1999 the acquisition was announced in *The Bookseller* (the unknown author mistakenly referred to as 'Michael Faber'). By now, US and French rights had been bought by Harcourt Brace and Le Seuil respectively; a lucrative film option was being negotiated too.[14] Already there was a sense at Canongate that *Under the Skin* had uncommon potential. But its editorial process was not without challenges.

The copy editor, Helen Simpson (not to be confused with the acclaimed short-story writer of the same name), was asked to provide notes on the manuscript, and she responded detailing significant reservations. In feedback to Moir, she confessed to being 'desperately worried', fearing that 'if the book goes out in its present form it will do serious damage to Michel's reputation'. She asked, 'Would Michel be willing to do a major overhaul, do you think? Or, would he refuse, believing that everything's fine and dandy?' In Simpson's view, the root of the problem might partially have been in the form itself:

> Alas, I don't think Michel has done himself anything like justice with UTS. It's as though, writing in the longer form, he's lost the confidence and imaginative concentration that illumine his short stories. There are so many problems that it's hard to know where to begin.[15]

Those concerns ranged from plot holes to Isserley's backstory, a problematic relationship with antagonist Amliss Vess, even the underlying premise. Shortly afterwards, Simpson wrote a slightly toned-down version of her letter to Faber direct, asking him to reconsider.

His response to Simpson is fascinating, read now with the knowledge of how the novel was received. Simpson responded as a fan, thinking Faber, on the basis of *Some Rain Must Fall*, a significant talent. Some of the points she made regarding believability and plot holes ring true, even now. (According to Moir, this was Simpson's great talent – 'she was meticulous, which is why her skills were in demand from major London publishers').[16] So this was no ill-considered evisceration. Rather, her letters read now as genuinely anguishing – Simpson is worried for the author, and hopes to save him a harsh critical exposure. The discussion retains value 20 years later, as Simpson's report began a revealing conversation about storytelling itself.

In his reply, Faber accepted textual advice; he fixed some plot holes too, recognizing Simpson had improved his novel. Also, he noted she had read a slightly earlier version than Faber and Moir were now working with. But rather than argue back conventionally about this or that problem, rather he made a case for how novels work – or do not – for readers, on an emotional level:

> I knew, right from the planning stages of UTS, that the character of Isserley would connect emotionally with some readers and leave others cold. She is Everywoman – except, of course, to those readers for whom she is (literally and metaphorically) no woman at all. I could certainly imagine some people feeling she's one of *the* great characters of 20th century literature and other people feeling equally strongly that the book's glaring, fatal flaw is its ridiculous and unconvincing protagonist. If most readers end up feeling the latter, I'm prepared to take the knocks. In my alien heart of hearts, Isserley is realer than anyone can know.[17]

From an unknown writer to an experienced professional, that line imagining readers thinking Isserley 'one of *the* great characters of 20th century literature' reads like staggering confidence. Or perhaps a little defensiveness? Coming from someone who had worked so hard to lead readers *not* to expect autobiographical writing, in that line about his 'alien heart of hearts', Faber also made explicit the connection between protagonist and author. This was ultimately echoed in *Under the Skin*'s dedication, in which he thanked 'my wife Eva, for bring me back to earth'. Faber considered he *was* Isserley, and that her story was believable because, in some disguised way, it was his own.

In his response, Faber argued that in fiction, believability is a red herring. He listed the novels *On the Road*, *The Portrait of the Artist as a Young Man* and the then-recently published Scottish classic *The Trick is to Keep Breathing* as examples of celebrated, 'believable' books that left him cold:

> The protagonists [of these books] are supposed to *move* us. They don't move *me*, so I'm free to focus more closely on the text's shortcomings... in my experience, listening to people talking about books or films they have (or haven't) enjoyed, 'implausible' is usually a criticism that's levelled at a story when it's failed to connect emotionally. The same person who sneers, 'Come on, are we really supposed to believe this beautiful young girl would find a middle-aged bozo like Sylvester Stallone irresistible?' might have no trouble at all weeping along with Humphrey Bogart and Ingrid Bergman.[18]

Faber also pushed back on the matter of overall effect. Responding to Simpson's references to *Gulliver's Travels*, Faber said he was not trying to encourage readers to compare human and animal behaviours at all. (Some critical writing about *Under the Skin* still assumes this was Faber's intention.) Rather, '[i]n this book I was interested in nurture and exploitation, the psychology of slaughter, the frailty of sexual and human identity'. None of this was dependent on how many hitchhikers might realistically go missing in the Highlands in a short period of time, how much meat a single factory could produce, the administrational processes Ablach Farm might be subject to in Scotland. If readers were invested emotionally in Isserley's journey, he believed, those things would become irrelevant.

Ultimately Faber held his ground, with Moir's backing. In the Canongate archives, Simpson's letters are annotated, Moir's responses scribbled in margins – she was convinced that publishing was not risky. Reflecting on the process now, Moir recalls that the publication of *Under the Skin* was a defining moment for her personally, one of a handful of such experiences over a lifetime in publishing. Still, she might have wondered. If Simpson – an already sympathetic, sophisticated reader – read *Under the Skin* this way, would others see nothing but its 'glaring, fatal flaw'? Soon, they would all see.

## The Story

The opening scene of *Under the Skin* sees protagonist Isserley driving a red Toyota truck up and down the A9 road in the Scottish Highlands, wearing a low-cut top and looking to pick up male hitchhikers. Isserley drives past potential marks once before going back to have a second look. She wants to avoid 'weaklings', sizing men up like pieces of meat. Readers know neither who she is nor where she comes from, though her outsider status is clear. When she picks up a hitcher on his way south the language between them initially suggests flirtation, though not for long: 'what had seemed like growing intimacy between them hardened into mutual unease' (UTS 15). Readers are likely to be uneasy too. They may think they know Isserley's aim, though invented language in the novel's opening chapter destabilizes expectations. Isserley has access to an 'icpathua toggle', the 'trigger for the needles inside the passenger seat, to make them spring up silently from their little sheath-like burrows in the upholstery' (UTS 21). This knocks out whoever is in the seat, allowing Isserley to get her men back to Ablach Farm. At the end of the first chapter, that first victim passes out from the needles. The language used is undeniably sexual.

Early chapters suggest a realist novel with a fractal structure, patterns repeating themselves in different versions each time. Isserley searches for hitchers, lets them into the truck, then they talk while she tries to work out whether to let them out again. All the while, Isserley's internal monologue – deciding what to say, how to respond, how to manoeuvre her mark into position, how to avoid confrontation – charges the story. As Faber told Helen Simpson, the book was 'saturated with Isserley's consciousness', the author's preferred 'third person authorial voice' technique particularly well suited to this story. In her domain, Isserley seems vulnerable as she makes awkward conversation. When perspective occasionally switches to the hitchhikers' points of view, readers see her as some of her hitchers do: 'Women don't dress like that, he thought, unless they want a fuck' (UTS 34). Even as Isserley is presented as an attacker, readers are encouraged to fear for her safety.

Isserley is an anomaly on the A9 road: how, though? She considers herself to be 'at work'; she takes her job seriously and wants to do it well, though she is both physically uncomfortable and physically uncommon in a way the hitchhikers notice but find difficult to define. Isserley's behaviour suggests a predator trying her best to go unnoticed by the law. Certainly, she is obsessed by being careful. As she puts it, 'To act on impulse was to invite disaster' (UTS 35). She observes closely, finding much about the locals strange. She finds it hard to distinguish between these individuals, different as they seem to readers: 'Already he looked much like all the others she had picked up,' Isserley thinks, examining a victim lying prostrate in the passenger seat; 'later, when his clothes were all off, he would look more or less identical' (UTS 22). Readers may now expect her to kill these men. Though where she is really taking them is more shocking.

Increasingly, Faber's invented language is scattered throughout the narrative. Isserley refers to 'vodsels', a word which initially goes unexplained. She uses the word 'alien' in a curious context. The overall effect is of a slow, careful drip of information that undermines those initial expectations: that this is simply the story of a serial killer, bound to repeat her habits – bound, eventually, either to be caught by the police or become a victim herself. Isserley tries to avoid physical contact; on the rare occasion it happens, it fills her with fear. When one hitchhiker gets out, calling her a 'little Samaritan' for giving him a lift, he touches her without permission, 'squeezing her affectionately on the arm with one big hand before she realized what was happening. If he noticed the hardness and thinness of the limb, he didn't let on' (UTS 33). In every pick-up, the riskiness of her working life is reinforced. Eventually, readers learn the truth. Isserley drives a victim to Ablach Farm, where her co-workers await, to enact the next part of the process. Here, 'vodsels' are stripped naked, their tongues removed, access to language denied – then they are taken down below ground, with the others.

Seen in her small living space on the farm, reader assumptions about Isserley are complicated further by how she is seen to suffer when alone. This is because of the surgery she has been forced to undergo before coming to Earth. She had a metal rod inserted through her spine; she finds it uncomfortable to remain upright for long periods of time. Isserley is a four-legged 'alien' who has been surgically disfigured in order to fit in among 'humans', having been given little choice over whether to accept this strange new life after escaping a place called 'the Estates'. Originally canine in nature, her tail amputated, even now Isserley grows fur that needs to be regularly removed. She learns local language and cultural references through her TV. She is deeply traumatized by her past, while her physical state – copied from a model in a men's magazine to make her as conventionally attractive to potential victims as possible – causes her continual pain. Her only solace is the stunning landscape of the Highlands itself. Despite all this, Isserley does not doubt the value of her work.

Soon, the drama of the novel moves to the impending arrival of Amliss Vess at Ablach Farm, which puts Isserley and her co-workers on alert. Isserley considers Amliss 'the most beautiful man she had ever seen' (UTS 110), though readers know their understanding of 'man' must be re-thought, as must words like 'human' and 'animal', inverted in this world. Amliss is the wayward rebel heir to Vess Incorporated, Isserley's planet's only distributor of 'voddissin', a meat made from the bodies of hitchhikers, a kind of in-demand, expensive rarity. After the first third of the novel has been coy about the rules and culture of this fictional universe, both suddenly become undeniable.

Vess has travelled to Ablach Farm secretly to see things first hand, horrified by where voddissin comes from. He insists upon seeing the vodsels underground; Isserley must take him down there. Readers might expect to find her sympathetic to the suffering of others. On the contrary. She insists to Vess that vodsels do not have emotions, cannot communicate, unlike their own people. When a vodsel draws in the sand, desperately trying to appeal for mercy, she pretends the message means nothing, though she understands it perfectly well.

From this point on, the thriller-like pace of the novel increases. Vess sees an opportunity and sets four vodsels free, sending Isserley and her boss into a panic: they must catch the vodsels before they are found by anyone else, the whole farm exposed, their entire enterprise at risk. They find, shoot and kill the escapees, but Isserley is changed by the experience, her faith shaken. Soon after, the risk readers have been aware of throughout is realized in all its horror, when Isserley picks up a man who forces her at knifepoint to have sex with him, this being the chapter Faber had wanted to dodge with ten blank pages. Dramatically, Isserley kills her attacker. Shocked by the attack and her own capacity for violence, she escapes. Isserley becomes more reckless, picking up her next hitchhiker without the care and attention she knows is critical. The end is coming. By the time she delivers her next victim to Ablach Farm, she can no longer deny the commonalities between herself and her victims. Feeling guilty that her last hitcher's dog was trapped in his van, she goes back and frees it. (Even now, she feels a greater affinity with dogs and sheep than vodsels.) She decides she will never go back to the farm, or this work. Having picked up one final man, now nervously driving too fast, her Toyota collides with a tree, the hitcher thrust through the car's front window. Her own body is once again transformed, Isserley realizing in a daze that 'her spine must be shattered' (UTS 292–293). In a moment of fleeting connection, a strange woman finds the wreck, encourages Isserley to stay calm, then heads off to get an ambulance, promising everything will be alright. Isserley urges her to take the hitcher; he's still alive, and she knows what will happen if his body is not removed right away. But the woman cannot understand. How could she? After she leaves, Isserley reaches for the 'aviir' button which will 'blow her car, herself, and a generous scoop of earth into the smallest conceivable particles' (UTS 295). The novel ends with a sublime description in which Isserley fantasizes over what awaits her. Uniquely for Faber, it represents both tragic and happy ending in one, lyrical as anything in the author's oeuvre, in which his most isolated, loveless character sees an opportunity for community – with the landscape itself, imagining her future:

> The atoms that had been herself would mingle with the oxygen and nitrogen in the air. Instead of ending up buried in the ground, she would become part of the sky: that was the way to look at it. Her invisible remains would combine, over time, with all the wonders under the sun. When it snowed, she would be part of it, falling softly to earth, rising up again with the snow's evaporation. When it rained, she would be there in the spectral arch that spanned from firth to ground. She would help to wreathe the fields in mists, and yet would always be transparent to the stars. She would live forever. All it took was the courage to press one button, and the faith that the connection had not been broken. (UTS 296)

In the author's most stunning finale, the presence of the words 'faith' and 'connection' in the final sentence's final clause stand out. Having been forced to face the work she does and its consequences, also her commonality with other beings, there is only one escape left for Isserley.

## THE BOOK OF STRANGE NEW THINGS

If *Under the Skin* is a novel about an alien on Earth, *The Book of Strange New Things* might be described as a novel about a human becoming alien on another planet. In this third part of 'Faber's World of the Novel', I make a case for *The Book of Strange New Things* being Faber's most successful exploration of faith, delivered with compassion and a morally conscious outlook informed by the writing of previous novels. A look at process is revealing, particularly given the book was written as Eva was dying. This forced the husband-and-wife team into different worlds. In the novel, this is evident in the radically differing experiences of protagonist Peter, living on the faraway planet Oasis, while his wife Bea lives on an environmentally imploding Earth, each unable to fully experience the other's reality. In post-publication interviews, Faber described how Eva's cancer influenced the narrative's development:

> ...[W]hen the person you love has cancer and you don't, they really are on a different planet; they are on planet cancer. And you can love them, you can support them, but you can't really *be with them*. So that all fit into the book. Saying goodbye to all the things the book says goodbye to was also saying goodbye to Eva. And she helped me with that book a lot. She helped me to edit it and to finish it.[19]

In order to fully appreciate *The Book of Strange New Things*, then, it is necessary to acknowledge Faber's personal circumstances. The following study details the nature of this novel, its context and reception, personal life being indivisible from creative decisions taken on the page. This chapter finishes with a look at Part One of the novel, also the role of the Oasans themselves, interrogating each of these for evidence of Faber's compassionate approach in action.

## Reception and Context

By any measure *The Book of Strange New Things* must surely be considered a success – both critically and commercially well received, it was quickly and widely translated, and its reputation has only grown since initial publication in 2014. Promoted more squarely by Canongate as sci-fi than *Under the Skin*, Faber received his first nomination for the prestigious Arthur C. Clarke award for Science Fiction Book of the Year, as well as winning the Saltire Society Scottish Book of the Year in 2015 – a rare combination. (That year's strong Saltire shortlist included Andrew O'Hagan, Irvine Welsh and Janice Galloway.) *The Book of Strange New Things* was soon adapted into a ten-part BBC Radio 4 series. Amazon Prime also aired a pilot of a TV adaptation, called *Oasis*, in 2017, starring Richard Madden (Robb Stark in *Game of Thrones*), though this was not picked up. Still, these were signs of Faber's growing reach as a writer, capable of sustaining that uncommon mix of critical acclaim and significant readership, while re-inventing himself once more. It may seem now like this novel's impact was inevitable, but it was a risky endeavour. Often, Faber wanted to give up on it.

He began writing *The Book of Strange New Things* in 2008, after a rich creative period. In the previous four years three Faber books had been published: *The Fahrenheit Twins*, *The Apple* and *The Fire Gospel*, his 'medium-sized' story which attempted, like *A Photograph of Jesus*, to encourage readers to take faith seriously. *The Fire Gospel*, a creative response to the myth of Prometheus, was published as part of the multi-national Canongate series The Myths. This was one of Jamie Byng's ambitious ideas which saw novellas from hugely renowned writers, such as Margaret Atwood, Phillip Pullman, David Grossman, Milton Hatoum, Su Tong, A. S. Byatt and Dubravka Ugrešić, produce new takes on world myths. Faber 'usually preferred to write what moved him', but he had been working on *The Fire Gospel* already – and what moved him fitted the series well; when Byng approached Faber for a contribution, he agreed. The story was simple: obscure academic Theo Griepenkerl stumbles upon a previously unseen 'Fifth Gospel' in a destroyed Iraqi museum, plundering the text written by Malthus (who claims to have been present when Jesus died on the cross), then publishing it with his own introduction.

The 'Fifth Gospel' becomes a worldwide sensation. Soon, Theo is in danger, being kidnapped by men who are, for contrasting reasons, horrified by the book's impact.

This context matters to *The Book of Strange New Things*. Firstly, because Faber had been strongly against the 2003 invasion of Iraq, and had written the story partly as a response to it, though it also poked fun at the changing, Amazon-drenched, publishing industry. While writing *The Fire Gospel*, Faber also penned a rare non-fiction essay, 'Dreams in the Dumpster, Language Down the Drain', published in *Not One More Death*.[20] This 2006 anthology featured Harold Pinter, Richard Dawkins and John le Carré, whose essay title, 'The US Has Gone Mad', gave a sense of its contents. Faber's anger and upset were clear: 'We writers operate on the assumption that language matters,' he wrote. 'And then we're endlessly slapped in the face with evidence that it doesn't. Actions speak louder. And violent actions speak loudest of all.'[21]

Around this time, Faber withdrew from public life. His family was now financially secure due to the success of *The Crimson Petal* and *Under the Skin*, so he had the rare freedom to refuse to self-promote – but this withdrawal was rooted in a genuine disgust at political events, which would feed into *The Book of Strange New Things*. Years later, after re-engaging again, he was open about the ways in which his frustration over the wars in Iraq and Afghanistan led him to want to write a different kind of book: 'I was so fed up with the almost invincible idiocy of the human race that I fantasised about writing a book that had no humans in it. So I was going to write a novel entirely set on another planet.'[22] (Eva wasn't sure, seeing the move as likely to put off readers.)

But this was only part of the picture. He was also driven by his ongoing desire to write about faith. His last attempt had not worked for everyone. Though he was proud of it, *The Fire Gospel* was that rare thing, a Michel Faber book with a genuinely mixed reception. Theo was seen by some readers and reviewers as an unlikeable, shallow protagonist written without much nuance, while Malthus came across as either wilfully naïve or plain foolish. In discussing *A Photograph of Jesus*, Faber has compared that book's believers to Theo's kidnappers – 'cartoon characters' readers might be unlikely to empathize with. In this context, then – disgusted by war, reclusive and starting a new project when his latest story of faith was, as he saw it, misunderstood – Faber embarked on a big new novel, keen to erase the humans. But as ever, a Faber novel changed in the making, once again because he decided he wanted a particular emotional effect. In 2008, Eva was diagnosed with cancer of the bone marrow, and the novel became about an unusually strong love, under unusual pressure. He still made aliens critical to the narrative. He did not avoid portraying alien life as a real, physical thing, the vulnerable Oasans (who cannot recover from their illness) being described in precise, otherworldly detail. But the idea of cutting humans out entirely was discarded.

As if it wasn't enough to attempt a big, interplanetary sci-fi novel featuring multiple alien characters, replete with their own impossible-to-render language (Canongate worked with the author to invent this), Faber was still looking for new ways to write. Unlike with his other very long story, *The Crimson Petal*, which was intricately planned, with *The Book of Strange New Things* he was interested in his writing process reflecting the protagonist's experience. With this novel following a man leaving Earth for an unknown planet, Faber 'wanted to go on the same adventure as Peter, and discover things as he discovered things'.[23] This meant a more fluid creative process, also one more likely to be influenced by what was happening in the author's life at the time of writing. Much of the work on *The Book of Strange New Things* was done when Faber felt the pressure of time, being urged to finish the book by Eva while she was ill and he was reluctant to work. Perhaps, then, it is no surprise to discover *The Book of Strange New Things* is a novel full of anxiety, well-meaning impotence and fragility. It is also a meditation on loss and the 'miracle of the body',[24] limited but magical as it is.

The period 2008–2014 was unusual for Faber, in that he published almost no fiction for six full years. It is tempting to assume this was purely down to Eva's condition. There is some truth in that. But *The Book of Strange New Things* is a 600-page book written as an extended experiment: as with all experiments, there were some things the author tried, then had to revisit because they were not working. Also, it is worth noting that over the six years Eva had cancer, there were periods of hope, remission, despair – and she remained her husband's constant collaborator for most of this time.

As long as she was well enough to join him, Faber resolved at Eva's urging to start taking up invitations again, ending his self-imposed retreat from public life, starting once more to travel for book festivals, tours and residencies when international invitations came in. This meant they could see more of the world together, knowing their time was limited. (Eva had a form of cancer she was unlikely to defeat in the long term.) Meanwhile, as with *Under the Skin* and *The Crimson Petal*, whenever he got stuck or they thought there was a problem with *The Book of Strange New Things*, Eva wrote out passages to help Faber then draft sections in his own words. He remembers her contributions to some of the most evocative sections in the novel. The specifics were always his; he didn't utilize her prose and she did not ask for or expect it. These exercises were provocations – ways of working out the challenges of the writing process as a team:

> [S]he wrote an account of what Peter felt during his first walk outside in Oasis, and also an account of Peter's early life with his parents, which fed into the chapter in the middle of the book at the end of which Jesus Lover Five interprets Peter's weeping in his sleep as a long song. Eva felt there needed to be a big glow of human emotion and Earth-connectedness in the centre of the book and complained when I'd sailed past the midpoint without one. So that whole chapter is there because of her.[25]

When Faber repeatedly credited Eva as his collaborator, he was not doing so out of politeness, guilt or duty. These were significant parts of the creative process, important to credit appropriately. Indeed, it seemed the longer they worked together, the more collaborative the process was becoming; this was only heightened by Eva's illness, with Faber often working on the book by her bedside. This is not to say they saw everything similarly: they disagreed on the character of Bea, who Eva found 'irritating and unlikeable'. Also, she wanted Peter to be 'more on the ball emotionally'. This was a particularly important element to get right. Faber remembers:

> It was a tricky balancing act in that book, because Peter had to be sufficiently 'OK-whatever' to pass USIC's screening process and fit

in with the amiable zombies at the base [his fellow USIC workers], but sufficiently human to realise in the end that he couldn't stay there and belonged with his own kind, so to speak. It was difficult to calibrate, but I think Eva's complaints helped to clarify what was & wasn't working/ringing true.[26]

This seems critical. Eva was not suggesting changes to prose or phrasing, she was thinking critically about elements such as structure, balance, emotional heart, how to avoid losing readers. In a book Faber described as 'about decency and goodness' which is 'difficult to write about in a way that well-defended worldly-wise agnostic readers won't find offensive or dull',[27] getting those elements right was an essential high-wire act. As was the business of the Oasans themselves: how to make them seem real without seeming ridiculous? This novel would surely stand or fall on whether readers bought into the idea that they could exist, in this way, in this imagined place; also that they could find the 'corny' presentation of Christianity moving, life-affirming, enduring.

## Narrative Beginnings

*The Book of Strange New Things* is a novel in four parts, the four connected titles (Part I: Thy Will Be Done, Part II: On Earth, Part III: As It Is and Part IV: In Heaven) each drawn from the verse Matthew 6:10 in the King James Bible. This is no accident; neither was the placing of the quotation, which appeared indented and in all capital letters, almost invisible, under the jacket of the first edition: 'I AM WITH YOU ALWAYS, EVEN UNTO THE END OF THE WORLD...' (also from Matthew, 28:20). The novel's structure and presentation both foreground not just faith in general, but specifically Christian faith, and its capacity to be a vehicle for enduring love. The chapter titles suggest connective tissue between each part of the story too, each title being made up of the end of the final sentence of the chapter in question. Even the overall title of the novel suggests this interconnectedness, the 'Book of Strange New Things' being the name the Oasans give to the Bible. And not just any version, but the King James.

This novel follows Peter, a well-meaning 33-year-old preacher and recovering alcoholic who is selected by a company called USIC to travel to a faraway planet, Oasis. His job is to minister to the indigenous communities there. Part I opens with him travelling to the airport, where he will say goodbye to his beloved wife, Bea. Peter and Bea are both believers who run a local church together. Bea made it part of the way through the USIC selection process; they wanted to go to Oasis together, but Bea did not make the cut. After some deliberation, they decided Peter should go alone on this extraordinary interplanetary mission in the name of Christ; Bea would run the church at home, living with their cat Joshua. (Yet again, humans find their most powerful connections are often with non-humans in Faber – and Bea's connection to Joshua is vital.) While Peter is away, they will be able communicate using a 'shoot', a kind of old-fashioned letter-writing computer system (it has no other functions at all), which has been installed in their home on Earth as well as in the room Peter will be sleeping in.

From the outset, Peter and Bea are presented as not just being devoted Christians but also as good people – 'they seldom missed an opportunity to show kindness to strangers' (BSNT 5) – but on their way to the airport, Bea is restless when Peter suggests they pick up a hitchhiker. (This represents another inversion of *Under the Skin*, which also opens on the road, passing someone who needs a lift – though this time, there is no malice involved.) Bea tells Peter this is their last chance to make love before he leaves. He is uncomfortable, but she wants him one more time and they have sex in the car – later in the book, this becomes an important moment. In fear and hope, Peter soon departs from the airport, devastated to be parting from Bea, but sure in the value of his mission. Most Faber characters spend a lifetime searching for a single moment when they might find a connection worth holding. These two have had it for years, every day. Peter asks himself, '[W]hat was he going to do without her, out in the field?' (BSNT 12). Can they survive the vast distance about to open up between them? From their first interaction after the parting, technology acts as a barrier between them. Their first phone call cuts in and out. Already, they are losing each other.

The journey in a rocket to Oasis takes a month, during which Peter is knocked out. This process is referred to as 'the jump' by

Artie Severin and BG, his companions, who have been to Oasis before, are going back there, and know what's coming. As the IV drip kicks in, Peter passes out, petrified: '[H]is greatest fear, as he dissolved into the dark, was that he would never see other humans the same way again' (BSNT 38). As premonitions go, this one is pretty accurate. He awakes on Oasis, being welcomed by a woman called Grainger, another key character. Soon, he gets acclimatized to the USIC base. Everyone here serves several different useful work functions – apart from Peter. Everyone here is single and has few connections back on Earth – apart from Peter. Exceptions have been made to get him here.

Ultimately, Peter is on Oasis to work with indigenous Oasans: he is determined to treat them as equals, even to serve them, as they wish to be served, in the name of Christ. Even when he hears from Grainger that she's not sure they want to be known, he just grins: 'Nevertheless, I'm here to know them' (BSNT 75). For Peter, every simple meeting with a new person is a genuine search for understanding (this will lead him later in the novel to learn as much of the Oasans' language as he can). Every memory is an attempt at connection. Belief is treated with seriousness and respect. When Bea, in her first letter back to Peter sent through the shoot, tells him to '[t]rust in Jesus. He has made the journey with you' (BSNT 95), readers are not encouraged to laugh but to urge him, with Bea, to draw strength from their common faith, as it will steel them both for the unknown that lies ahead.

Many novels with love at their heart are propelled by some kind of breakdown in the central relationship; in this case, the love remains strong initially, before being thoroughly shaken; the distance between the lovers grows ever larger with the passage of time, despite their efforts to prevent that. Peter keeps saying he is not good with written communication – in person, he has a natural talent for respectful, effective communication, even with those at the base who think his position ridiculous or who demean the Oasans' settlement, calling it 'Freaktown'. But through these letters – Bea is an articulate, furious writer, sending detailed, passionate missives from Earth – readers notice what Peter cannot: that he is not really listening. In the excitement of his mission (Bea reflects that he seems to be the most fortunate, most well-treated missionary in history), he cannot truly engage with the awful avalanche of tragic environmental news coming from Earth. Grainger, whose job it is to take Peter to and from the Oasan settlement, believes the problem is not with the individual, but with the epistolary form itself: 'Writing stuff down so as the other person can understand it and then waiting for an answer is a nightmare' (BSNT 91).

In Peter's early days on Oasis, readers wonder, as Peter does, if he is about to discover some malevolent intent on the part of USIC. He seems to have been brought here to support the Oasans, who were desperate for a new minister, having lost their old one. Ever the politically correct missionary, Peter is conscious of the tropes, the potential assumptions and pitfalls for a man in his privileged position. In another echo of the concerns of *Under the Skin*, assumptions regarding the creaturely are often undermined or subverted. 'We're the aliens here,' says Peter (BSNT 104), shortly before he meets an Oasan for the first time.

When he finally does, Peter is dazzled by the Oasans' innocence, their generosity, their keenness to learn the word of God from The Book of Strange New Things.[28] The community of believers, or Jesus Lovers as they name themselves (each has only a number, no name, and little to distinguish between them except the colour of their robes), are humble, kind, sensitive and generous to a fault. But can they really be? Throughout these exploratory sections of the novel, the author was as surprised by the development of the plot as any future reader, much of the tension coming from a potential or imagined shock or betrayal it often seems is about to be revealed, but which never comes. Meanwhile, if readers are waiting to discover Peter's own dark side, this also is suggested, but never developed. On the contrary, Peter remains highly aware of his responsibility to the Oasans, continually checking his behaviour and language. Later in the novel he will choose to live among them rather than back at the base, to join in their rituals, to listen – all of which operates as careful, knowing misdirection. As Faber wrote in 2022:

> It's my most exotic mis-en-scene [sic], to create maximum intrigue. There are so many red herrings in the novel to keep you continually expecting USIC to reveal its evil agenda or the Oasans to become

suddenly deadly – a variant perhaps on those old cartoons of the Christian missionary ending up in the cooking pot of the 'savages' he'd hoped to convert. Instead, the 'enemy', the 'deadly threat', ends up being our own human limitations, our powerlessness against bad luck, our lousy communication, the energy we pour into the wrong things.[29]

Each time readers think some awful betrayal is about to be revealed, it is not. And yet Peter, in his naivety and thoughtlessness, still causes Bea great pain. Just because he means well does not mean he protects himself or anyone around him from pain. Peter tries his hardest to be generous with others at the base when he is there. He resists making assumptions about them, and does not force his faith on anyone. Having planned to simply spend some time getting to know the Oasans during this trip he is staggered by their already strong love of Jesus; seeing this, he puts his energies into re-writing biblical passages so they are easier for Oasans to pronounce and understand, even making up copies of the scriptures himself, DIY, so his growing congregation don't have to share.

Meanwhile, Earth is hurtling towards catastrophe. Every time Bea writes to Peter, there is a huge new disaster to tell him about, though he cannot fully appreciate from his faraway vantage point what this means. When she reveals her pregnancy to him, he cannot compute it. (They conceived on the way to the airport – though Bea did not tell Peter she stopped taking birth control. This is a rare moment of purposeful deceit in the novel, one she asks forgiveness for.) Though Bea is desperate for him to be happy about this news, to react in some way, Peter cannot even bring himself to mention the pregnancy in his letters. This human compassion machine, fully employed around the clock in the business of genuine goodness, generosity and kindness to all, makes his beloved wife feel betrayed by him through his carelessness. It is one of the most impactful elements of the novel.

The Oasans themselves warrant a direct look. Faber's approach to narrative structure (attempting to write a novel made up of well-meaning actors, trying to do right by each other) has been widely commented upon, as has Peter's role as minister. In this chapter overall, I have argued that Peter is the most successful embodiment yet of Faber's lifelong effort to write compassionate fiction that encourages readers to engage seriously with matters of faith. But Peter does not operate in isolation. Rather, as we have seen, his compassion is observed primarily through his thoughts, behaviours and responses to others. Typically for Faber, the author does not restrict these responses only to other humans – but to animals (Joshua the cat plays a crucial role, so too do the 'animals' on Oasis) and to the Oasans themselves. This is not an occasional or marginal element in the novel's makeup, rather a sustained effort, central to the narrative.

One temptation in the writing was to make the Oasans look absurd to human eyes; Faber rejected this, instead giving the Oasans a dignified physical look that encourages readers to treat them as Peter's equals. In *The Book of Strange New Things*, Oasans wear long robes and hoods, 'like monks', these robes being the only way that at first glance Peter can distinguish between them. (In time, with effort, he learns which robes correspond to which 'Jesus Lover', the names and numbers they choose for themselves.) Oasans do have two arms and two legs of a kind, also a torso, though these are covered by robes, and their language, voices and 'heads' defy human understanding. This provides a huge challenge for Peter, as he tries to work out how to 'look' at them in the way they might wish to be seen.

As Faber intended, the reader goes on the same journey as the author did in the novel's making, discovering the Oasans and their world in surprise after surprise. Peter describes meeting his first Oasan like this: 'His voice was soft, reedy, asthmatic-sounding. Where the s's should have been, there was a noise like a ripe fruit being thumbed into two halves' (BSNT 121). In fact, Peter goes on to question his own use of 'should', also of gendered terms – he cannot tell if Oasans have any conception of gender in their society – and soon he lets go of these initial assumptions, as he learns to understand which sounds in English are difficult for them to pronounce. The 'face' of an Oasan is more challenging, even for someone like Peter. In fact, he cannot make out anything he understands as a face, and even struggles to look at Oasans direct at first, so uncomfortable is he with what he sees. But again: in time, with practice, he is able to make meaningful connections with Oasans, despite the classic Faber 'unbridgeable gap', made vast in this case.

Though Peter is continually trying to understand what Oasans want and need, how he can support them, how to avoid offending or upsetting them, he keeps coming up against the fact that in terms of language, culture and their view of the realities around them, there are many things he simply cannot understand. And yet the continued attempt – in all its flaws – is what drives forward this story which is so unusual, being absent of any traditional antagonist, any familiar sci-fi trope or device that might set Peter against anyone. In my view, this is the major achievement of *The Book of Strange New Things*: it manages to retain tension and narrative thrust over 600 pages, despite there being no enemy, no fight, only the will to try, in good faith.

At the end of Part I, Peter arrives at the 'C-2' settlement, where he will meet the whole community of Oasan Christians for the first time. When he arrives he finds a huge sign, in English, made by the Oasans to make Peter feel one of them. 'WEL COME,' it reads. As Peter takes in this kindness, he notices groups of Oasans coming out of their homes, into the landscape. They are singing, in unison. Eventually he realizes, falling to his knees, that they are singing the song he most associates with what he considers corny, naff, Salvation-Army Christianity, something that in any other context he would struggle to connect with. 'I once was lost and now I'm found,' sing the Oasans as one (BSNT 177-178). For Peter it is real and powerful, and it brings him, in gratefulness, to his knees – united in faith and compassion with strangers of another species.

# 4

# Faber's World of *The Crimson Petal*

Any book considering Michel Faber's work must give requisite space to the author's most successful novel, *The Crimson Petal and the White*. But this book was not a one-off, rather one part of a compelling pair, along with *The Apple*. One book is fat, the other thin. One is widely read, the other barely. One is a novel set in a single year, the other a disparate collection of stories crossing centuries. But there is strong connective tissue here. This chapter examines the writing process for *The Crimson Petal*, provides a narrative summary, then reflects on the book's success and Faber's resistance to writing a sequel – resistance which led to *The Apple*.

*The Crimson Petal and the White* was written, mostly, in three bursts. The first of these began in 1979, when the author was an undergraduate at the University of Melbourne. During this time he spent months 'in the Baillieu Library's satisfyingly gloomy "B" wing, reading as much primary material as I could find... I had Victoriana coming out of my ears.'[1] Research, then, was a part of the process from early on – and he was studying Victorian literature on his course. But Faber's attitude to research was influenced by what he later called the postmodern 'literary climate' of the time:

> ...[M]y relationship with accuracy and anachronism was somewhat cavalier. I regarded history as an old curiosity shop to be plundered, not in any sense as a circumscription of my options. My characters were free to join political parties that did not yet exist, read books that had not yet been written, travel on non-existent train lines, and pay ten times too much or too little for common purchases. It

was history's job to inspire me, not to frustrate me or oblige me to investigate anything I found dull.²

The years 1979 and 1980 saw much progress on this 'cavalier' early version, Faber sketching a dramatis personae detailing names, ages and character relationships which would remain remarkably consistent from then on.³ He drafted 100 pages, then got stuck. The second burst came seven years later, Faber completing a full draft in 1987, when he was a young nurse – famously, this version had a tragic ending for his protagonist, Sugar. He thought the novel complete, then left it alone.

The third burst, in late-1990s Scotland, saw the manuscript transformed. Faber has repeatedly credited Eva with this, who advised him on everything from character to plot. (It was Eva who argued against the tragic ending, while the character of William Rackham was originally 'more villainous', at Eva's urging becoming 'more complex and more likeable, making him more villainous still'.⁴) The novel might not have been published without her advice, or had the same impact. The eventual ending became a much-noted strength, one Thomas Oberender called 'the greatest shift in voice since Dostoyevsky's *Crime and Punishment*'.⁵ But off-the-page factors were at play too. An unknown author would have found it near-impossible to find a publisher for such a book; Faber was no longer unknown. Canongate wanted as much fiction from him as they could get.

Timing was also crucial. In October 2002, the same month *The Crimson Petal* was published, Yann Martel's *Life of Pi* won Canongate the prestigious Booker Prize, giving them new international reach. To date, *Life of Pi* has sold ten million copies. Jamie Byng bought UK and Commonwealth rights to it after meeting with Faber's US publisher, Ann Patty. (Patty was the acquiring US editor for *Life of Pi*, and had a copy lying on her desk when Byng was in New York to discuss *The Crimson Petal*.) In 2002, Canongate also won UK Publisher of the Year, an unlikely feat for a then 'tiny independent publisher'.⁶ If there was ever a time to publish a vast, explicit, wildly ambitious Victorian novel with Canongate, the end of 2002 was it. In a sign of the publisher's ambitions, Byng insisted on printing an unheard-of 1,000 proof copies. The copy in the publisher's catalogue was not understated: 'a major work that truly rivals the finest Victorian novels for breadth, depth and sheer reading pleasure'. Meanwhile, a major London launch was arranged in Trafalgar Square, packed with significant industry figures. The launch was a huge success, and – though it was not a bestseller in the UK (one critic on BBC2's *Newsnight Review*, Rosie Boycott, said she threw the book at a door) – soon Faber was No. 1 in Italy, France, Holland and a bestseller on both the *New York Times* and *LA Times* lists. German rights were bought for an extortionate amount. By now, Faber was a major international writer, and as Judy Moir recalls, 'we all knew, this was the big one'.[7] But how did it go from those cavalier early versions to the final, polished manuscript?

## THE MAKING OF

When Faber embarked afresh upon *The Crimson Petal* in Scotland, much in his life had changed. Letters between Faber, Judy Moir and Jamie Byng suggest the writer was originally sending chapters to his publishers piecemeal during 1999, as he felt satisfied with them, once *Under the Skin* had been accepted. Conversations between writer, editor and publisher about the book continued through 1999. On 2nd November, Faber finally sent a full draft. The prospect of securing another Faber novel so soon was attractive to Canongate, especially one with clear commercial potential. That said, it was clear 'the monster' needed work.[8]

Editorial work began to gather pace in early 2000. On 15th March Faber wrote to Byng, tongue somewhat in cheek, asking for help with historical accuracy: 'I'm sure you'll find just the right reader... Maybe a very, very old female historian with a healthy interest in hardcore pornography. No worries, as they say in Australia.'[9] Judy Moir found Dr Kenneth Fielding, historian and 19th-century specialist at the University of Edinburgh. One letter to Fielding listed what Faber felt needed to be tackled most urgently: areas such as degrees of urbanization and suburbanization in London, money, wages, modes of payment, accessibility of the novel's settings, even what constituted a 'house' or 'flat'. Faber also asked Fielding to tell him what was missing from his London. Well-informed readers would no doubt notice them by their absence. In his letters, Faber used that word 'cavalier' again, in reference to old versions of the manuscript, stressing his keenness, now, to get period detail right.[10]

This work made for a significant improvement, but in a detailed letter in August 2000, Fielding explained he still had major concerns. Responding to the author's many queries, he wrote: 'geographically, I feel a real lack of local expertise'. Faber took Fielding seriously. By November 2000 he was also corresponding with the London Topographical Society's Roger Cline about St Giles, the area Sugar grows up in. Cline explained what houses were made from, when they dated from, potential dangers in the area. He wrote: 'Our heroine would have no need to fear Jack the Ripper anyway, as he operated a couple of miles to the East, around Aldgate.'[11] All this as Moir and Faber exchanged notes on the vast, changing narrative. Others contributed too. Helen Simpson provided feedback, though again Moir tried to protect Faber from this, and again Faber resisted many of her suggestions that came to him via Moir. Meanwhile, the walls of Faber's study were papered 'with original Victorian maps of London'. He joined 'online forums [such as VICTORIA] to geek up on everything from weather reports, lavender harvesting and treatments of the time for female hysteria'.[12] By now, all previous reticence about research was long gone – and for *The Crimson Petal*, it was essential. Faber has no sense of smell: having chosen a perfumer as a male lead, he needed that research to present those lavender fields convincingly.

During this time, discussions were ongoing over characterization. Given the unusual size of the novel, also the hugely detailed internal lives of the characters and often many pages at a time focalized through one individual before switching perspective, this was a significant editorial challenge. Because Faber disliked the phone and Moir preferred sending written editorial notes, much of this process is documented in letters or emails. Future scholars will find much worth exploring, not least the discussion of the character of Henry Rackham, brother to William.

As late as December 2001, they were still discussing what Faber was trying to achieve emotionally with Henry. As in other contexts, Faber was once again facing the challenge of how to write an intelligent, sympathetically rendered Christian who would not alienate or seem comical to agnostic readers. Henry was naïve, self-deluding; he was intended to work in contrast to William, but Faber remained concerned. He wrote to Moir: 'I want the reader to accept that Henry is good – which makes Henry's self-disgust at his "monstrous" nature all the more sad, because we know that compared to William he really is an angel.'[13] The editorial process was therefore not just about correcting mistakes, narrative inconsistencies, writerly tics; it was about the moral heart of the book. Throughout the process, Moir wanted more of Henry, requesting another chapter focused on him even at the end of the process; exhausted, Faber declined – or tried, and felt unable. He would return to Henry again, for *The Apple*.

By early 2002, by which time editorial work was nearly complete, *The Hundred and Ninety-Nine Steps* and *The Courage Consort* had both been published. Suddenly, Faber had a significant catalogue of work, all of it well received. One letter from Faber to Moir responding to *Crimson Petal* notes shows that even this audience-shy writer was not immune to praise:

> I'm back from London... all through the week I was away it was difficult to open a newspaper without seeing a review of *Consort* in it. And today I open the Sunday Times and see that one of the judges of the Impac prize is praising *Under the Skin* and Antoni Libere's [sic] *Madame* as wonderful literary discoveries.[14]

Readers may sense the writer's excitement; the attention must have seemed dreamlike. But Faber's editor soon brought him back to earth, sending a long list of *Crimson Petal* clichés she couldn't stomach – a sign they were now dealing in microconcerns. By March, the jacket was dominating Faber's thoughts. He hated the suggestions, especially those with a close-up petal – he even posted Canongate the strikingly similar cover of the masturbation guide *Sex for One: The Joy of Self-Loving* by Betty Dodson PhD to make his point. A month later, in an email titled 'cliché surrender', he wrote to Moir, 'Once more, the monster is vanquished.' Soon, most clichés were history, and the monster was, finally, off to the printers.

## THE STORY

*The Crimson Petal and the White* takes its title from the opening line of Alfred Tennyson's 1847 sonnet, a 'seduction song'[15] titled 'Now Sleeps the Crimson Petal'.[16] Faber later described his novel as 'an 835-page tale set in 1870s London... [that] follows the progress of a young woman, Sugar, a prostitute who longs to escape the influence of her abusive mother' (TA ix). The Gothic literature scholar Matt Foley has noted the novel contains multiple Gothic elements, but also, typically, it subverts several other genres too – horror, romance, comedy, tragedy. Initially the story is told by an all-seeing narrator who later drifts in and out, sometimes commenting on events, sometimes directing readers' attentions this way or that. At times, readers may forget this narrator exists as they pull close to a particular character, seeing what they see, thinking what they think. Elsewhere, that intrusive voice re-announces itself, all the while presenting itself as a kind of promise: to show the reader a good time.

In one sense, *The Crimson Petal* is Sugar's story: the novel documents her move into, and ultimate fall from, polite society. Certainly, she is the novel's protagonist. In another sense, though, she is just one character in a richly realized world which, from the first page, portrays Victorian London through the experiences and thoughts of radically different characters who fail to understand or fully appreciate each other. *The Crimson Petal* is as much the story of William Rackham, heir to Rackham Perfumeries, and his tormented, child-like wife Agnes. Both are the focus of the narrator's attention in sustained passages where Sugar is backgrounded or entirely absent. (Some readers assume Agnes represents the so-called 'white petal' of the title to Sugar's 'crimson', though associations here are complex, roles often reversed.[17]) Henry Rackham and Emmeline Fox also take regular turns to be the focus, Emmeline's Rescue Society work playing an important part in the plot, while Henry's tragic story provides that stark moral contrast writer and editor were seeking. Through these many changes in perspective, *The Crimson Petal* is about the contrasts between the characters, but also the reader's expectation of being comfortable in a novel of this kind, an expectation undermined from the opening lines:

Watch your step. Keep your wits about you; you will need them. This city I am bringing you to is vast and intricate, and you have not been here before. You may imagine, from other stories you've read, that you know it well, but those stories flattered you, welcoming you as a friend, treating you as if you belonged. The truth is that you are an alien from another time and place altogether. (TCP 3)

From the outset, then, readers know that what follows is not comfortable, or familiar, or easy, as – the narrator suggests – other Victorian fiction is. The novel sets itself up as a reaction against Victoriana that ignores the unforgiving reality of a world sometimes romanticized. The back-street abortions. The filth and stench. The rank hypocrisies of so-called polite society. This world, readers are warned, is brutal, unforgiving and alien. That word, 'alien', so strongly associated with Faber, is rarely applied in discussions of this novel. But despite its myriad differences, *The Crimson Petal* has much in common with Faber's fantastic work. Like Isserley from *Under the Skin* or Peter from *The Book of Strange New Things*, the reader is thrust into a strange world whose culture, laws and behaviours are deeply unsettling, our protagonist disorientated by its very structures. Here is, after all, another Faber novel about alienation and the difficulty of finding true connection, just one wearing Victorian clothes.

The novel has five parts: 'The Streets', 'The House of Ill Repute', 'The Private Rooms and the Public Haunts', 'The Bosom of the Family' and 'The World at Large'. The narrative takes multiple turns, but the overall structure is simple. *The Crimson Petal* can be traced through Sugar's journey from Mrs Castaway's house, via William's patronage, first into a home of her own, where she is kept as Rackham's mistress, then into William's own household, where she becomes governess to his neglected young daughter Sophie. The novel's settings move from 'the very bottom: the lowest of the low' (TCP 4) into more rarefied parts of London. The narrator is explicit about this journey, encouraging readers to see themselves in the role of someone who must seek to somehow gain a foothold in this society:

> What you lack is the right connections, and that is what I've brought you here to make: connections. A person who is worth nothing must introduce you to a person worth next-to-nothing, and that person to another, and so on and so forth until finally you can step across the threshold, almost one of the family. (TCP 4)

Eventually, that is what Sugar will be, 'almost one of the family'. Over the course of the book she transforms into 'Miss Sugar', a woman with a role, responsibilities and the promise of respectability. But that prospect is dependent on one man's approval. When Sugar loses that, she loses everything. By the novel's end, she has been exposed once more.

**Part One**

The novel opens on Church Lane, St Giles, just a few hundred yards from 'the opulence of Bedford Square and the British Museum', in an area that 'has more whores living in it than almost any other street in London' (TCP 4). Like most women here, Caroline, the 'nothing' who will introduce us to Sugar's 'next-to-nothing', has no prospect of escape. The fact that she was once 'respectable', a 'manufacturess of waistcoats and trousers' (TCP 13) shows how the women of Church Lane end up there. By no fault of their own, rather by the injustice of a society in which they have little agency, but which damns them as shameful nonetheless.

Caroline and Sugar have not seen each other in months. In their interactions, readers notice Sugar's determination to escape her circumstances, though it is luck that will allow her to do so. Soon, readers meet William. Self-important and deluded, though, thanks to Eva, not entirely unsympathetic, he is a hugely privileged man with growing money troubles. His father wants him to take over the family business, though he has shown no interest in it or aptitude for the task. Having been given the pamphlet 'More Sprees in London' by friends Bodley and Ashwell, which advertises the services of sought-after prostitutes, William becomes intrigued by Sugar, this girl who, legend has it, is an 'eager devotee of every known pleasure' (TCP 83). 'More Sprees in London' suggests clients search her out at a place called The Fireside. William gets lucky; he finds her, and over drinks they discuss literature. Sugar has taught herself to read and write. To someone like William Rackham, who thinks himself well-read, being able to quote from Shakespeare is part of Sugar's appeal. He dreams of being a celebrated writer, which is what he pretends to be when they meet, using the name George W. Hunt as cover.

Their first night together is no romantic encounter. William soils himself in her bed, in his drunkenness, and she has to clean him up. The language used to describe the sex between them that follows is – as seen throughout the novel – determinedly unsexy. Having been tricked into prostitution as a girl by her mother, Mrs Castaway, Sugar despises her life. (In secret, she is writing a novel about a prostitute who violently attacks her clients.) When she swallows William's semen, it is described as 'warm gruel', his penis a 'scrag of gristle'. The imagery leaves the reader in no doubt – readers are not being encouraged to invest emotionally in this relationship. At the close of Part One, Sugar is in the bath, finally free of her clients for a short time, 'Emperor Pisspants' among them: '"God damn God," she whispers, tensing and untensing her pelvic muscles, "and all His horrible filthy creation."' After her ritual cleansing, in the mirror she sees 'an angry young woman ready to murder anyone or anything that stands in her way' (TCP 124). No wonder.

**Part Two**

At the start of Part Two, one thing is clear. William Rackham is obsessed:

> He inserts a cigarette between his lips and sucks a naked flame against it, reconfirming the decision he made almost immediately after leaving Mrs. Castaway's; that he must have Sugar entirely to himself. An idle dream? Not at all. He need only be rich, and wealth, great wealth, is his for the claiming. (TCP 127)

In this way, an explicit connection is made between William's future success and his motivation for that success. It is not pressure to conform, nor a sense of responsibility to his family, nor a desire for financial stability that changes William, rather a single night with Sugar.

In the following chapters, the dysfunction of Rackham House is made plain. Agnes, treated as mentally ill and thoroughly incapable by her husband and the servants, has something in common with Mrs Castaway: Agnes does not acknowledge the existence of her daughter Sophie, who has been literally hidden from her since birth, within the walls of a home that traps them both. Dr Curlew, brother to Emmeline, regularly visits Rackham House, urging William to commit his wife to an asylum. Curlew is another villain who resists reductive readings. On one hand, he seems hell-bent on getting Agnes sectioned. On the other, his motivation seems at least in part to come from a belief she will return fully recovered and capable of enjoying motherhood. In *The Crimson Petal*, no character is completely honest or dishonest. Rather, all are complicit. In a story Faber consciously made as a moral, humane 'feminist deconstruction of the patriarchy' (MFCE 2), readers are urged to invest in them anyway. Soon, William returns to Mrs Castaway's to propose he pay to ensure Sugar is his alone. Intoxicated by lust, he realizes he needs to show himself his father's worthy successor if he is to afford this new, secret life. With Sugar's support and encouragement, he sees 'his debts vaporise and his assets multiply' (TCP 194).

Henry, by contrast, hates the family business, resents capital and loves Emmeline, though the two cannot admit to their love. Rather, they conduct chaste walks after church where they discuss potential meanings of scripture. Emmeline educates him in the nature of her work at the Rescue Society, where she reaches out to the sex workers of London. (Routinely, they reject her.) Henry is shocked but fascinated. He admires Emmeline's work, but distrusts his own instincts. He fears straying from his path. When Emmeline becomes ill, Henry suffers untold torture; his piety prevents him from admitting his desire.

By the end of Part Two, William has sourced a new home for Sugar in Marylebone, where he plans to conduct their affair, away from the dirt of St Giles and the judgement of Mrs Castaway. As he pushes Sugar down onto her new mattress after surprising her with the new place, he thinks of 'the trouble he went to in choosing the furnishings, the rare and elusive objects he found'. He says nothing of this to Sugar, though. 'It's better this way, not to puncture the fairytale magic of his gift' (TCP 268). Though what follows reminds readers of William's selfishness, and how unlike a fairy tale their story is, this section does end on a celebratory note. Readers might be forgiven for forgetting how they met. Once William is gone, Sugar struggles to believe this is real. '"Oh dear God," she sobs, "I'm *free!*"' (TCP 272). But Sugar's new relative luxury is conditional. Realizing this, she resolves to make herself more essential to William's business. Alone in her new home for the first time, she reflects on her change of circumstances; in the morning, she will 'have to suffer, for the first time in her life, the unmitigated rawness of a new day' (TCP 274). In a sense, she has moved from one house of ill repute to another. Though at least this one is more comfortable. And it has its own privy.

**Part Three**

The start of Part Three sees Sugar once again damning God and all his creation, after a brief, depressing visit to Mrs Castaway, who resents her daughter's good fortune. At this point William has been absent from Marylebone for weeks, and Sugar must fill her time; is she free to do as she pleases? Or is she obligated to be in this one spot, should he decide to visit his mistress?

When the narrative switches, readers understand why William's focus has been elsewhere. The religious Agnes, forced to give up her beloved Catholicism on marrying a Protestant, thinks an angel 'from the Convent of Health' (TCP 289) has waved to her from the street, and will soon come to rescue her. This leaves William frustrated, confused. The picture of respectable Victorian femininity in a way Sugar could never hope to be, Agnes is idealized by William but is ignorant about society, also her own body. (Menstruation was never explained to her; she considers her monthly cycle to be evidence of the devil within.) No one listens to Agnes; even her maid Clara patronizes her. But she *has* seen someone. Sugar has taken to following her, spending her otherwise empty days trailing the Rackhams. Sugar was the waving angel Agnes saw at her window.

When they are reunited, William's desire for Sugar appears undimmed, though he swears he loves Agnes; he sees no betrayal in his affair. For him, Sugar's feelings are irrelevant, though he does seem dedicated to making a life with Sugar while also looking after his wife, anguishing over whether it is morally right to send Agnes away. As William's obsession grows, so too does Sugar's obsession with Agnes. In one key scene, she follows her to a performance of Verdi. When Agnes runs from the theatre after vomiting over William's friend Lady Bridgelow, Sugar runs to protect her in the street. Once again, her angel has come. She promises to return.

The parallel narrative concerns the 'handsome and high-minded' Henry (TCP 377), who has become increasingly fascinated with the prostitutes of Church Lane himself. Hopeful of impressing Emmeline while she recovers from a bout of consumption Dr Curlew predicts will kill her, Henry wants to do some rescuing of his own. His love of Emmeline weighs heavy, and he is incapable of appreciating the lives of the St Giles women. Finally, desperate and wild, believing Emmeline is dead, Henry burns his Bibles in a fire and ends up burning himself to death, fantasizing during his last moments about uniting with Emmeline in the afterlife.

This interleaves with Sugar's own story when she attempts her most audacious pitch so far. On a visit to the Rackham lavender fields, when William laments their lack of time together and the recent resignation of Sophie's governess, Sugar suggests she take the job herself, bringing her closer to William and a more secure living situation all in one. Enticingly, this will also put her and Agnes under the same roof. In a scene loaded with tension – at any moment, William might cast her back onto the street for such insolence – Sugar gently broaches the subject, barely able to cope with the thought of what she is about to do. The passage is unusually lyrical for Faber: 'Her breath wheezes, her tongue feels swollen with lavender, the earth on which she stands is beginning to revolve, like a giant piece of flotsam on an ocean too vast and dark to see.' At first, it seems Sugar may have gone too far: 'William's face is distorted in the firelight, his eyes reddened by conflagration; his flame-yellow teeth are bared, in amazement – or outrage' (TCP 493). Sugar thinks, 'Dear Heaven, his lips are curled in disgust...!' Then William receives news of Henry's death, which arrives via a messenger in the field. In a hot flush, Sugar faints.

## Part Four

Henry's death changes William. Having initially recoiled, he now agrees to Sugar's suggestion, and she enters the Rackham home, this mysterious place where 'men are unhappy and women are driven mad'.[18] Newly installed as Sophie's governess, Sugar has to improvise – she has few conventional skills. She is well read but cannot play music or speak other languages. She has little idea how to prepare a young girl for a society she has been shut out of, except in the pages of books. But no one is watching. Sophie was neglected by her previous governess, who insulted her and showed no affection. Beatrice underestimated her charge. Sophie soon adapts, and she and Sugar become close. (For both, this is their first experience of a genuinely loving relationship.) Agnes, meanwhile, suffers in another room. She has an undiagnosed brain tumour. The medication Curlew gives her makes her worse, and his 'examinations' (heavily hinted as being sexually abusive) cause her untold distress. Her hallucinations become more potent, though some visions are real. After all, her angel is now living in the house and has stolen her diaries, retrieved after Agnes buried them in the garden, hoping for a fresh start.

'The Bosom of the Family' sees Sugar reading Agnes's diaries. In Faber, letters sometimes promise meaningful access to a character's inner life, though the contents are as likely to obscure meaning. Sugar finds Agnes's diaries inane, impenetrable, though she cannot look away. The more she reads, the more fascinated she becomes. But at Rackham House, Sugar does get access to a life she was previously denied. She is even included in the Christmas celebrations, receiving a present of Shakespeare volumes from William in full view of the servants, and observing the family games with Sophie (who is usually kept upstairs on Christmas Day, as on all days, to ensure Agnes does not have to see her.) Faber presents this seasonal celebration as heart-warming but also as a kind of denial – not just by the family, who facilitate Agnes's avoidance of Sophie while patronizing and abusing her, but also a denial of the world outside the household. Emmeline has no interest in denial, which is why, when Agnes approaches her thinking she has miraculously recovered from consumption after a visit to the 'Convent of Health', Emmeline does not indulge her. But Agnes has seen her angel, and believes she will be rescued.

## Part Five

Under renewed pressure from Curlew, William finally agrees to send Agnes to an asylum. Temporarily, he hopes. Sugar is horrified, suggesting to Agnes in a secret appearance as her 'angel' that she run away instead. Which she does. Soon after, a body is found in the Thames. William thinks the long-haired woman is his wife, though the woman's decomposed state leaves this unclear, and Sugar thinks Agnes has escaped. (Readers know Agnes cut her hair before leaving, suggesting this body is not hers.) In grief, William behaves ever more erratically. At times, he is cold with Sugar as he spends more time with Lady Bridgelow, who has been present throughout, feigning concern. At other times, William appears to be preparing to welcome Sugar into the family. In an apparently hopeful scene, he takes Sugar and Sophie to a photography studio, where a family portrait is taken of the three of them. Sugar allows herself to imagine a future as William's wife, before realizing with cold certainty that she is nothing to him, and never will be: as she discovers, he replaces Sugar's head in the resulting 'family' photograph with a cut-out photo of Agnes. The Rackham family of three were never in the same room, until now. 'Stupid girl,' Sugar scolds herself, acknowledging her true place.

In the final chapters of *The Crimson Petal*, the surviving characters' situations turn more desperate. With Agnes gone and William distressed, Sugar, already vulnerable, realizes she is pregnant. Knowing this can only lead to expulsion from the house, she throws herself down the stairs. William initially shows care, but changes his attitude when learning of the pregnancy after an examination by Curlew. Shut out by William, Sugar has to resort to writing to him.

In Faber, letters hold power; they can suggest closeness or distance, an attempt to connect or a disinterest in connecting. In this case, the formality of Sugar's dismissal by letter proves there is no way back into William's affections. When she writes in appeal, insisting she is not pregnant and begging to see him, she gets no reply. 'How dare he do this to my child,' Sugar says, hugging Sophie, when William tells his daughter she will once again have a new governess.

Having lost the approval she worked hard to build, Sugar must escape to survive. In haste, she decides to take Sophie with her. What she plans, readers do not know – maybe she does not know herself. In the dash to leave, Sugar's novel (which she has not added to since her time at Mrs Castaway's) flies away behind her on the street. Discovering fragments of this after the fact, William misunderstands the contents, also Sugar's reasons for departure. Full of moral outrage, he heads for Church Lane, where he expects the 'explosive denouement' he feels he deserves – 'the revelation, the release of tension, that will shake the universe in fierce convulsion, and then allow everything to fall back into its rightful place, restored to normality!' (TCP 830). But nothing here will be restored as William wants it.

In an echo of the novel's opening, readers are returned to Caroline, as she helps an injured William catch a taxi. (He hurt his leg badly during his frantic search, having ignored Caroline's warning to watch his step on her stairs.) At the end of *The Crimson Petal*, the main narrative questions are left unresolved, though readers know William has lost his wife, mistress and daughter due to neglect. The novel finishes with him feeling betrayed, seeing himself as an upstanding man beset on all sides. In these final pages, there is an increasing sense of time running out – the narrator reappears to warn that soon, readers must leave this world. We are thrust once more into the darkness of the 'shabbier creatures' of Church Lane: 'Let them toil, let them grub, let them disappear into obscurity, you haven't time to see any more' (TCP 830). Then, suddenly, the novel is over. Does Sugar survive? Does Sophie? Where is Agnes? With one more flourish, the narrator re-enters the narrative to say farewell, with a hope that readers leave *The Crimson Petal* satisfied – or at least, having been shown a good time.

## RECEPTION

The response to *The Crimson Petal* was ecstatic and immediate. In the years since, the book's reputation has only grown – in 2011, the BBC made a successful mini-series with standout performances from Romola Garai as Sugar, Gillian Anderson as a wonderfully sour Mrs Castaway, and Richard E. Grant as Curlew. It continues to be Faber's most celebrated book. But how was it perceived at the time?

In September 2002, before it was even published, James R. Kincaid of the *New York Times* noted the evident tropes of earlier Victorian writers, but sought to situate the book in a different tradition:

> The novel is likely to be hawked as another retelling of *Jane Eyre* because it presents us with yet another madwoman and yet another attic, along with a host of tough and resilient women. But it's not the shadows of Brontë or even Dickens that are cast over this world; it's that of the later and darker Victorians, Trollope, James, Meredith, Hardy and George Eliot. These are the realists who, as James said of Trollope, helped the heart of man to know itself better.[19]

Kincaid argued readers were put in the role of stalkers with a moral purpose. He linked this to Faber's prioritizing of sympathy, a kind of resistance of judgement Kincaid argued was also a feature of that period's best realist writing:

> Faber teases us into making mistakes, almost forcing us to make easy judgements and indulge in stereotyping... The narrator sets himself up as our guide, offering little lectures on the scenery and exploring the innermost thoughts of the characters, as if both were of equal interest and transparency... This device, so reminiscent of the great Victorian realists, allows us the space we need to exhaust our knowingness and move past satire and into that haven carved out by 19th century agnostics: inescapable sympathy. This sympathy is neither sentimental nor observed; it is seeded and nurtured. Gradually, the novel's direct address disappears and we are allowed to make our own way, to find feelings and states of being we didn't know we possessed.[20]

Where the likes of Kincaid focused on the moral, other reviewers read *The Crimson Petal* as voyeuristic, seeing the narrator as emblematic of this. In interviews, Faber described voyeurism as something conducted passively, at a distance, whereas he aimed to give all his fiction 'genuine warmth',[21] something he believed could only be achieved by refusing to flinch in the face of harsh realities. Another review, written by historian, biographer and Victorian-era specialist Kathryn Hughes, argued the value of the novel was in its approach to presenting that reality:

> Michel Faber has produced the novel that Dickens might have written had he been allowed to speak freely. All the familiar tropes

of high-Victorian fiction are here – the mad wife, the cut-above prostitute, the almost-artist, the opaque governess – but they are presented to us by a narrator with the mind and mouth of the 21st century. Where once the Victorian novel was lace-like with decorous gaps and tactful silences, now it is packed hard with crude fact and dirty detail.[22]

That review has been oft-quoted since, including by Faber himself. Meanwhile, *Time* magazine also concentrated on the 'dirty detail', celebrating *The Crimson Petal* for its presentation of the realities of the period:

> We're used to holding the Victorian period at a distance in sepia-coloured photos and carefully art-directed Merchant Ivory productions, like a fragile heirloom grandma told us not to play with, but Faber's language seizes it roughly, takes us into the drawing rooms and up the petticoats, and shows us people putting a brave face on the private pain of life.[23]

How strange for Faber, after all those years of recoiling from the prospect of an audience, to find it in such dramatic fashion with a novel begun, as a teenager, with none in mind. The *Time* review in particular is interesting. Despite its questionable tone (it encouraged readers not to be put off by 'the author's ominously French-sounding name'), reviewer Lev Grossman linked Hughes's 'dirty detail' to the 'private pain of life' shown through all that sympathetic rendering of the inner lives of flawed characters. In *The Crimson Petal*, all the main characters get internality, compassion and empathy. Even rapists get the chance to present the world as they see it. In William Rackham's rape of Agnes, Faber does not recoil from the undeniable fact of his oppression, nor her lack of consent; neither does he recoil from William framing this cruelty and abuse *the way he perceives it*. As readers, we are not encouraged to deny the violation. But we are forced to recognize that William sees what he does as a loving act between husband and wife.

One way internality finds its expression in *The Crimson Petal* is through characters' various writings, Agnes's diaries and Sugar's novel being prime examples. Agnes's diaries range from her teenage fantasies of an idyllic future marriage to her desperate anguishing years later, when she dreams of being rescued by her angel. Sugar's writings, by contrast, are what Matt Foley calls 'revengeful resistance fantasies' (MFCE 168). He argues that her novel in progress, *The Rise and Fall of Sugar* (or *Men vs Women*), can be read as a 'particular flight of Gothic fancy':

> Indeed, her visceral and pornographic stories seem to be sublimations of her traumatic circumstances under the care of Mrs. Castaway. Even amongst the most squalid and exploitative of conditions, her literary 'flights of Gothic cruelty' provide a medium through which Sugar may pleasurably imagine herself as a subject with absolute agency. (MFCE 168)

Using fiction as a way to 'pleasurably imagine' another life is seen in the act of reading as well as writing. It is no coincidence that on their first meeting, Sugar tells William her favourite Shakespeare play is the 'gory frenzy' of *Titus Andronicus*, Shakespeare's revenge tragedy 'of rape, mutilation and cannibalism' (MFCE 169). At this point, there is a connection between Sugar's need for reading and writing this kind of material and the fact that in real life she must act the supplicant.

Once Sugar's material circumstances improve, she finds it harder to access that visceral desire for revenge that allowed her to imagine the fictional murders of her clients – something Caroline cannot help but notice. By the time she lives with the Rackhams, she feels distanced both from her novel and from the woman who wrote it. She cannot abandon the book, those pages scattering accidentally to the winds as she and Sophie depart Rackham House forever. But she no longer takes pleasure in imagining others' 'private pain'. Rather, she has undergone another transformation, one perhaps less obvious but more fundamental than that of prostitute to governess. By the novel's end, she loves someone unconditionally, uncomplicatedly. Or as the author put it himself, 'There is every reason to hope that Sugar, damaged though she undoubtedly is by her past, will not perpetuate the cycle of abuse' (TA ix). Sugar's and Sophie's stories are cut off abruptly as they ride away on the omnibus, their future uncertain, but this is still far from the tragic ending Faber originally wrote decades before.

## THE APPLE: CRIMSON PETAL STORIES

*The Crimson Petal*'s success led to immediate calls for a sequel. Ann Patty, Faber's US editor, wanted one. Readers got in contact directly to appeal for one. Under pressure, Faber demurred. As it happened, he had already been writing more *Crimson Petal* fiction, producing two new pieces about Sugar and Emmeline respectively over Christmas 2002, one being issued as a limited edition chapbook in the US soon after. But Faber was not working on a sequel. Rather, he was putting together *The Apple*, which existed in a related fictional universe but which resisted conventional development of the narrative strands of Sugar, William, Agnes or Sophie. The stories of these characters all appeared to finish on question marks that left some readers complaining: 'Novels aren't just supposed to stop!' wrote one young man from Texas, in a letter Faber kept. 'Novels aren't like real life. Novels are supposed to have satisfying tight endings' (TA xii). Responding to this correspondence in *The Apple*'s Foreword, Faber argued his new book was not an answer to any questions readers might have from *The Crimson Petal*: 'We are still a very long way from knowing "what happened"', he wrote. 'These stories offer openings, not closure. Or if they offer closure, it is of an instinctive, emotional kind.' Readers, then, might view this approach as an expansion of the world of *The Crimson Petal*, rather than a continuation of it.

Though the stories expand that world in rewarding ways, reaching inventively across centuries both before and after the events of the novel, Faber could not have chosen a less commercially promising way to respond to his biggest success. Some who followed his publication patterns already knew he was ever committed to avoiding repetition; this approach did at least allow him to return to his beloved short-story form in a new way. *The Apple* was presented as being 'about characters who also appeared in *The Crimson Petal and the White*... The stories are, as stories should be, little worlds of their own' (TA xvi). These seven stories across time were:

1) 'Christmas in Silver Street' (in which, two years before Sugar meets William Rackham, *The Crimson Petal*'s narrator instructs readers to 'close their eyes', 'lose track of time' (TA 3) and join

a 17-year-old Sugar and brothel drudge Christopher sharing a chicken on Christmas morning);

2) 'Clara and the Rat Man' (in which, four years post-*Crimson Petal*, Agnes's ex-maid, now a prostitute, is forced to leave her 'once-cherished illusions and inhibitions' (TA 22) behind, joining the 'repulsive-peculiar' Mr Heaton in visiting a rat pit, where he expects her to insert an overgrown fingernail into his rectum);

3) 'Chocolate Hearts from the New World' (in which a young Emmeline Fox conducts her solo 'just and gentle' war against slavery, writing to slave owners in the US during the 1850s, appealing to their 'moral courage' (TA 63));

4) 'The Fly, and its Effect on Mr Bodley' (in which William's tired friend reconsiders his life choices, staring 'deep into the abyss of human futility' (TA 83) after becoming haunted by an insect on a prostitute's buttock);

5) 'The Apple' (in which Sugar chases barefoot and 'helpless with fury' (TA 100) after an evangelist at her window, having seen the woman strike her child for dropping an apple);

6) 'Medicine' (in which William Rackham, now in decline in 1890, reflects mournfully on his life with his still-idealized 'poor little wife' (TA 117) Agnes, and Sugar, the woman who 'wrote herself into his heart' (TA 116));

7) 'A Mighty Horde of Women in Very Big Hats, Advancing' (in which 92-year-old Henry, son of explorer and women's rights activist Sophie Rackham, narrates his memory of the famous Women's Social and Political Union march in Hyde Park in 1908, via his Edwardian childhood, his culture-shock relocation from Australia and the legend of the mysterious Miss Sugar, his mother's 'steadfast travelling companion during their exploration of the world' (TA146)).

These historical stories – six short, one medium-sized – may seem, on the surface, particular to the world of *The Crimson Petal*, though on closer inspection they reveal themselves as being reminiscent of other Faber worlds. Like 'Somewhere Warm and Comfortable', 'Christmas in Silver Street' is a vignette showing ordinary human kindness amid the 'reality of squalor' (TA 12). Like 'Nina's Hand', 'Clara and the Rat Man' is a bizarre Faber mini-drama about a fleeting connection, this one unachieved, between two body parts. 'Chocolate Hearts from the New World' is another Faber epistolary story, like so many others, one in which well-meaning characters in impossibly different worlds give each other the benefit of the doubt. Though they see Christianity differently and will never agree about slavery, Emmeline's Georgian correspondent nonetheless sends her 'sweet trifles... as a token of my gratitude for your interest in my soul' (TA 69). Like 'Toy Story', the title story of this collection is another tale about powerlessness and alienation, the violence Sugar witnesses representing an injustice she cannot help but rail against, but cannot affect. In this way, she is like the protagonist of 'Toy Story', who cannot be heard or seen by those she observes. By the end of the story, though, she takes her experience to be a lesson in necessary restraint: 'She'll never get out of Silver Street if she carries on like this. Only the steeliest resolve and chilliest heart will rescue her from a life of subjection' (TA 103). The events of 'The Apple' therefore teach Sugar a lesson she will need to heed when William Rackham stumbles into Silver Street in Part One of *The Crimson Petal*. 'The Apple' is also a reminder of Faber's feminist instincts. (Sugar complains that 'in every story she reads, the women are limp and spineless and insufferably virtuous. They harbour no hatred, they think only of marriage, they don't exist below the neck, they eat but never shit' (TA 95). Then she resolves to write her own story.) Meanwhile, 'Medicine' is another Faber study in male entitlement, showing William's compassion on the one hand while making clear his folly on the other.

The last story is unlike anything else. This is the most explicit advocation of women's rights in Faber's oeuvre, with Sophie Rackham coming as close to an uncomplicated Faber heroine as there has ever been. Suffragette, activist, traveller, moral crusader, loving mother – as her son tells it, she has it all (Henry is named after the original Henry Rackham, to whom she had a 'sentimental attachment' (TA 176)). Here is that happy next act for Sugar, too, if readers needed it. Though the young reader in Texas might not have his desired 'tight ending', he at least knew Sugar was not caught moments after *The Crimson Petal*'s final page. In this way, there is circularity at work in *The Apple*. 'A Mighty Horde...' even returns Sophie Rackham to the home she escaped as a 7-year-old, in an impulsive moment when she and Henry depart the march in Hyde Park.

Tonally, 'A Mighty Horde...' nods to *The Crimson Petal* several times, continuing a habit also present elsewhere in *The Apple*. For some, this may reduce the work: when Henry promises not to die before getting to the story of the march, saying 'I do understand how maddening it is to only get so far, and not know what happened next. I wouldn't do that to you!' (TA 170), readers might be forgiven for getting slightly irritated. Even the final lines of this story echo the narrator of *The Crimson Petal*, making promises of satisfaction, though this time they remain unfulfilled. 'Come back tomorrow, and I will tell you the rest. Everything you still want to know, I promise. Tomorrow' (TA 199). In a sense, Faber was refusing to give readers what they were asking for. Though he did not ignore those desires for closure; on the contrary, he kept referring to them.

This is also seen in the existence of that Foreword. Some reviews suggested the author felt the need to get his excuses in first. Maybe he was trying to forestall further pleas for closure. In it, Faber gave examples from the extensive correspondence he had engaged in with readers since 2002, many of whom wanted simply to know: what happened? The author explained:

> I grew tired of explaining that there was not going to be a sequel. Sugar has been denied privacy all her life, I would say, and by the end of the novel she has earned the right to make her own way in the world, unscrutinised by us. And isn't it fun, at the end of the book, to be challenged to do what the Victorians were obliged to do between instalments of serialised novels: construct what happens next in our imaginations? (TA xvi)

For Faber, then, this approach was partly about Sugar's exposure to us, as readers, and her freedom from that, also about the Victorian experience of reading in instalments. But Faber suggested his sudden ending was not all that sudden:

> Re-read the final chapters, and you will find that there is a gradual leave-taking, a drawing of curtains, a succession of narrative farewells to each of the key characters. Yes, their future is uncertain. But so are all our futures. Only death concludes the story, and

Sugar and Sophie are still alive. A sequel would crush that life out of them. (TA xvi)

No sequel, then. Instead, these stories which stand alone, but act in conversation with the novel. This is quite the trick, and though undoubtedly some readers were disappointed, three of these stories in particular, 'Clara and the Rat Man', 'Medicine' and 'A Mighty Horde...', did fill in important gaps, and certain parts of *The Apple* may yet send readers back to *The Crimson Petal*, wondering. In one seemingly inconsequential passage of the novel, William asks himself: 'Was that a smirk on Clara's face? Damn her impudence, the snotty little minx. He'll see her on the street yet, for this...' (TCP 592). 'Clara and the Rat Man' shows this comes to pass, with Clara cursing the 'pompous old windbag who'd dismissed her with a damning letter of reference so poisonous that she'd spent more than three years trying to get decent employment with it, only to be driven to her current line of work' (TA 53).

After *The Apple*, certain events are undeniable. For example, in 'Medicine', readers learn that William marries Lady Bridgelow. They learn that Rackham Perfumeries has become Rackham Toiletries, a name whose reputation has sunk so low that when a grown-up Sophie asks for Rackhams on her return to London in 'A Mighty Horde...', the shop assistant has not heard of the brand. In 'Medicine', readers see that 15 years later, William has still not found Sophie: 'Fate is cruel, fate is vicious,' he thinks. 'All one's overtures of love are rejected, all one's well-meaning is misunderstood' (TA 124). He torments himself with fears of what might have happened to Sophie: 'She might have given him a grandson to pass the business onto. She might, for all he knows, be working in a brothel, servicing drunken louts while Sugar sits counting the money. She might, for all he knows, be dead' (TA 125). Anguish blurs his vision. He can hardly bear it – but at least *readers* discover what happened to her. Undeniably, Sugar got away. Undeniably, she travelled the world. Undeniably, William had a grandson. Sugar even left behind an inheritance.

## ONE REGRET

Let us finish this chapter by returning in brief to Henry Rackham, the character Faber wrestled with so much during the editing process. At the end of his Foreword to *The Apple*, Faber asks: 'But why these characters, and not others? Why this slim volume, and not more? Because these were the tales that demanded to exist.' Henry, it seems, was more reluctant:

> My one serious regret is that I didn't manage to write a story about Henry Rackham, a decent man who deserved so much more than he got in *The Crimson Petal*. I offered him an opportunity to live again, as a younger person, even as a child; I urged him to seize the chance to say the things he'd been too shy to say the first time round. He remained too shy.
>
> Such things must be respected. (TA xviii)

Something, then, seemed incomplete for the author, too, as well as for his readers. Soon, he would return to the challenge of writing an intelligent, moral Christian man once more.

# 5

# Faber's World of Verse

*Undying: A Love Story* occupies a unique place in Michel Faber's oeuvre. It acts as a kind of magic trick – it documents a painful, slow death, then the grief that follows, while insisting on framing that process as a romance that remains undefeated at the narrative's close. It is a book of poems that is also an autobiographical narrative and a dedication to a single individual.

*Undying* may stand apart in terms of form, but it is connected to Faber's other work in important ways. As always, the collection was an attempt to do something, in formal and genre terms, that Faber had not attempted before. A first clearly autobiographical work, this was a series of poetic non-fiction portraits and self-portraits. Another hybrid, then, though less obviously so. There was also a tonal commonality; Faber's familiar, disarmingly plain, unflinching prose was this time set to narrative free verse. As we have seen, his creative process starts with a feeling. That may be a kind of refusal of something. In this case, Faber disliked what he labelled 'the evasiveness and sentimentalism of the way our culture handles illness and death and grief'.[1] With the publication of *Undying* he expressed a hope that, for those left frustrated by that evasiveness, his poems might provide a 'vicarious voice'.

## OVERVIEW

Though he 'wrote a few poems about other things' as far back as his teens, which he has recently called 'trivial and naff',[2] Michel Faber has mostly written poems about hospitalization, illness and death. His first was called 'Of Old Age, In Our Sleep', drafted in 1984 while he was a nurse. A meditation from the perspective of plural subjects, the poem presented a 'we' who do not 'fear to die, to ebb away', instead fearing 'endless days / of torture, / forced intimacy / with a body that is not our own'. The same year, he drafted 'Old People in Hospital'. Both poems were finally published 30 years later, appearing at the start of *Undying* as a kind of introduction. Back in 1984, the author kept the poems to himself. It was another 15 years before he wrote a third poem with the word 'old' in the title, 'Old Bird, Not Very Well'. In this, Faber was again in the role of observer, walking 'as if on eggshell', in this case documenting something 'even ornithologists / may never witness', a small animal 'standing upright *in extremis*', considering whether to attempt crossing the road.

It is no coincidence that later versions of these poems found their way into Faber's only volume of poetry, in which frailty is a central concern – though by the time he returned to the form, his role as observer was intimate in a different way. As detailed in the author's Foreword, written in 2016, *Undying* documents the illness and death of his wife Eva, who in the Acknowledgements to *The Book of Strange New Things* he called his 'closest and most insightful advisor and collaborator' since 1988 (BSNT 585).

In June 2014, Faber was living in the London hospital where Eva was receiving treatment for cancer of the bone marrow. One day, when they were feeling more hopeful about future treatments, Eva insisted her husband read 'Old Bird, Not Very Well' to her oncologist. In Faber's words, the oncologist 'chose to see it as a poem about living as well as about dying. Eva wasn't convinced. But anyway, poetry had entered that dismal, antiseptic room.' Soon after, Eva was in the last days of her life, Faber caring for her night and day, a nurse once more. While she slept, Faber worked on the final edit of *The Book of Strange New Things* on Eva's laptop. There and then, he quickly drafted two 'alarmingly grim' poems, 'Cowboys' and 'Nipples'. He remembered the scene in his Foreword, two years later:

> I wrote only these two poems, and then it was time for Eva's cancer to kill her.
>
> Afterwards, as I tried to cope in a world that did not have my dearest friend in it, I wrote more. Sometimes none for several weeks, sometimes five in a day. I hadn't known such need for poetry before. I wish I'd lived into my nineties, with Eva at my side, and never written these things. (ULS 2)

But he had, and this was the result. Beginning with 'Old Age, In Our Sleep', now given new force in this context, these poems were presented not in order of writing but in a chronology that traces Eva's illness, death and aftermath. The Foreword suggested these were old-fashioned confessional poems about a very specific, real-world situation – but they were also a kind of rebellion. The Foreword argues that Eva is present in every poem. The writing of the book itself, after all, was an attempt to prevent her erasure. The evidence is right there in the title.

Though *Undying* is a book of poems, it is also a narrative collection, a capsule in time from the author's life, presented as a largely chronological story. This takes readers from Eva's diagnosis in 2008 through to her death in 2014, and into Faber's grief (not some alter ego, or narrator, or character, but Michel Faber himself), struggling to come to terms with his reality. The book is presented in two parts, the first 'tracing the terrible galloping course of Eva's illness, the destruction of the body, and the narrowing of life'; the second, Faber's attempts after she has gone to 'adjust to his new bleak reality'.[3] As nearly all the poems were written after she died, the author went back after their initial composition in order to make a more coherent narrative, as a novelist might, shifting new poems about the couple's meeting, life together and diagnosis earlier, while those written at her hospital bed, 'Cowboys' and 'Nipples', were pushed back.

The poem 'Lucky', placed third in the collection, sets the tone, subverting reader expectations of love poetry by repeatedly juxtaposing familiar romantic language (e.g. 'I looked into her eyes') and situations (holding hands, making love for the first time) with painful imagery drawn from the latter stages of Eva's cancer. The single long, irregular stanza moves from one juxtaposition to the next like a wince-inducing call and response. The poet will not let readers see 1988 without 2014 in mind:

> I looked into her eyes, and did not see
> the dark blood that would fill them when
> the platelets were all spent.
> All I saw was hazel irises, keen intelligence,
> a lick of mascara on the lashes she would lose.
> I thrilled to the laugh that pain would quell

> Admired the slender neck before it swelled
> and, when she gave herself to me,
> I laid myself against a cleavage
> not yet scarred by venous catheters.

In this way, the poet suggests, his own memories are intruded upon by what was to come. This mixing of romantic tropes and the harsh physical realities of cancer persists throughout the book.

Both parts of *Undying* are populated with narratives that might fairly be described as very short stories, though these cluster more clearly in Part One. In '[indecipherable] kappa', the 'best doctor in our area / went into the woods one day / and blew his head off'. The doctor 'liked you a lot / I think he was a little in love with you'. As the poem progresses, the poet wishes the doctor's 'ardour had been more profound' – enough to prevent his suicide, allowing him to be the one to diagnose Eva, in a more humane way than what she experienced. (The title of the poem refers to the scrap of paper thoughtlessly handed over when she first learned about her diagnosis.) Other poems also read like verse chapters. Though 'Switzerland' is barely a few lines, it suggests a potential whole other narrative, a route the story could have taken but did not – as Dignitas did not reply to Faber's tapped-out email request. These poems stand alone but are designed to be read in conversation. A poem like 'Switzerland' is charged, in part, by the poems that surround it.

In the early stages of the illness, Faber feared not having the strength to be able to cope with the coming horror. As such, 'Helpmeet' represents a point of paralysis that was eventually moved beyond. It is also an important poem in terms of what came after – beyond the last page, as it were, of *Undying*. In 'Helpmeet', the reader observes this changing in action. 'Broken and remade, I was what I had vowed / I could not ever be: your rock.' In being able to face the worst after all and support Eva to the end of her life, this gave him freedom after her death. He may have been in anguish, but did not feel guilty; that perhaps he could have done more, or somehow wasn't good enough for the task.

In Part Two of *Undying*, Faber passes through the rituals of grief. He must politely listen to offers of help while inwardly railing at the injustice of it all ('Don't Hesitate to Ask'). He wonders what on earth to do with Eva's living things (most notably in 'Your Plants' and 'Our Cats No Longer Miss You'). This section feels more universal than Part One. The book may be made in Eva's name, written partly to draw attention to her life. Though there is also a sense, in poems like 'Don't Hesitate to Ask', of something more about the poet than the subject, something that, even in its bitterness, is suggestive of Faber's compassionate approach to literary creation.

'Don't Hesitate to Ask' was selected for the Best Scottish Poems series by the Scottish Poetry Library in 2016, which that year was edited by Catherine Lockerbie. Lockerbie noted the poem's 'sheer linguistic violence', calling it 'a white-hot howl of fury at the insane injustice fate or God metes out and our pallid, useless politeness in the face of it'.[4] It stands out, being one of few moments where the poet drifts from the real world of inescapably mundane grief into the kind of imagined, fantastic world more commonly seen in Faber's novels:

> Well,
> actually,
> since you offer,
> yes:
> Would you mind driving me
> headlong through the universe
> at ten million miles an hour,
> scattering stars like trashcans
> scorching the sky?
> Put your foot to the floor,
> crash right through the gate of Fate,
> trespass galaxies, straight over
> black holes and supernovas
> to the hideout of God.
> Wait for me while I break
> down the boardroom door
> and drag the high and mighty fucker
> out of his conference with Eternity,
> his summit on the Mysteries Of Life,
> and get him to explain to me
> why it was so necessary
> to torture and humiliate
> and finally exterminate
> my wife.[5]

The poem's final line contains no question mark, though the question is implied. In this railing against politeness, amid the request to 'scatter stars like trashcans', the 'trespass' and the breaking down of doors, permission is not being requested for anything. When the author was invited to respond to the selection of the poem, he wrote of his experiences dealing with the small kindnesses of others:

> It [their home in Fearn] was an isolated spot and I'm not a driver so naturally neighbours, friends and acquaintances offered various kinds of support. It is, of course, lovely when people offer you a lift into town or a cup of tea. And useful too. But the poem addresses the impossible gulf between such gestures and what you truly feel you need when you've just lost the love of your life. Most poems that address death and grief are elegiac and dignified, wrapping up the pain in garlands of beautiful verse. That's fine for those who want that. This poem is for those who want something else.[6]

This response is revealing. *Undying* certainly includes elegiac elements. In places, it deals in dignity. Though few who read the book could accuse it of wrapping up the pain in 'garlands of beautiful verse'. Rather, Faber insists on looking without compromise at what love can be, in life and in death. Once again, the author has returned to his most common subject: the 'impossible gulf'. Though here, it takes a different form.

## RECEPTION

If short stories usually find fewer readers than novels, then poems usually find fewer readers than either. The same often goes for reviews. As neither a regular reader of contemporary poetry nor particularly engaged with that world in any meaningful way, Faber was seen by some as being not really a poet, rather a prose writer briefly dipping into poetic waters before stepping back out again. Canongate do not have a poetry list and were publishing the book because of their long-standing arrangement: whatever Faber wrote, they would publish. So most of the endorsements on the hardback came from high-profile novelists or thinkers, rather than other poets. (The first edition came with a quote from the novelist Ian McEwan – highly celebrated, certainly, though no poet, no expert in the field.) The potential audience for this book was readers of Faber's other books, or people interested in grief, rather than readers, necessarily, of poetry. This was evident in the critical response. *Undying* was named Poetry Book of the Year by Bel Mooney in the *Daily Mail*, a publication not known for its poetry criticism. (After the death of her own son, Mooney became co-founder of the Stillbirth Society, later re-named SANDS. She has a long-standing interest in literature about grief.) Notably, a good deal of the attention *Undying* garnered was through articles or features in national newspapers rather than specialist literary pages or poetry journals, mostly as part of interviews discussing Faber's grief, his writer's debt to Eva, his personal situation.

Faber's name helped garner attention. Allan Massie, in *The Scotsman*, called *Undying* a book that 'defies death', placing Faber in the long tradition of novelist-poets, comparing these poems to those Thomas Hardy wrote after his wife died, speculating this sudden rush of poetic inspiration may have been 'Therapy? Consolation? Who can tell? Necessity anyway.'[7] Interestingly, the review was credited not to an individual at the time, but to 'The Newsroom'; it was presented as a news item, not a straight book review. The novelist Michel Faber had been writing about the death of his wife: this was of more general interest than, say, the approach of the poems themselves, taken in isolation.

This reception was seen in microcosm in the interview Faber conducted with *The Guardian*'s Justine Jordan, who had been reviewing Faber's work for years, praising the likes of *The Courage Consort* in the past. Rather than assessing Faber as a poet, Jordan portraited Faber as a 'changed writer' trying to adapt to life without his long-time editor and who now took Eva's red leather shoes to his readings. Jordan drew a line from his major previous works to this new one in terms of the tone, so familiar from vastly different creations:

> From his debut novel *Under the Skin*, about a homesick alien hunting hitchhikers in rural Scotland, through his no-holds-barred neo-Victorian epic *The Crimson Petal and the White*, Faber has been a writer of singular vision who combines a dark, offbeat sensibility with an unnerving directness of tone – and the poems are no exception.[8]

That directness can be disarming, both in conversation and on the page, given just how uncommon it is, at least in a British context. In Jordan's assessment, part of what marks Faber out, regardless of genre or form, is his refusal to look away or sentimentalize, whether in an imagined industrial human-meat production line or a Victorian drawing room. In a book about the horrors of how cancer can ravage a body and traumatize both the subject and the subject's partner, that through-line is clearly evident. Faber's trademark delivery, often resisting the temptations of metaphor, instead favouring merciless, cool description, is arguably the most notable element of this study in care.

Any assessment of *Undying* must acknowledge that the author himself *chose* to present the project as an homage to a particular individual rather than a case for a kind of poetry, or a series independent of its subject. For Faber, the process of making these poems was more about Eva than the poems themselves. Indeed, as he'd stated so baldly in the Foreword – 'I wish I'd never written these things' – the author has no appetite at all for returning to the form.[9] And yet, if *Undying* was a project that seemed a complete dedication, interviews for the book suggested this was just a beginning to other kinds of dedication.

# 6

# Faber, Out of Time: A Look Back, A Look Forward

Any book about a writer composed during the subject's life must deal in speculation. What will they do next? Which projects are underway? What makes a look forward in Michel Faber's work intriguing is that it is also a look back.

As we have seen, from *The Crimson Petal* to *The Book of Strange New Things*, many Faber works have a long genesis, the author often working on several pieces simultaneously. Ideas, such as the intention to write, somehow, about music, might gestate for decades before picking up pace. Abandoned stories tend to get picked up years later. After *The Book of Strange New Things* was published, Faber stated he would write no more novels, some interpreting this as a kind of retirement announcement. Certainly, he was evaluating his circumstances. Eva had just died. He declared his need for solitude, and was leaving Scotland. And yet he has worked consistently since. At the time of writing, Michel Faber is in his sixties. He may work for many more years. In our correspondence in 2022, he laid out six projects in progress. The one thing we can be sure of here is: they are likely to change. How, we cannot know, but it is interesting to wonder. This final chapter represents a quick glance across the writer's desk, considering recent work and unfinished projects, which may one day see the light.

## *D: A TALE OF TWO WORLDS*

The first of these is complete. Typically, *D* originated in another novel begun in the 1980s, which Faber returned to after Eva's death. This book, published in 2020, is a fantastic fable for young adults which further develops Faber's ongoing interest in kindness on the page, and the lives of outsiders – another book about 'a stranger in a strange land'. Again, it was inspired by political events.

Given the widely noted declaration that Faber would write no more novels, it came as a surprise when a new one was announced. Still more so that this was Faber's first non-Canongate volume in the UK, instead being published by Doubleday, an imprint of Transworld. Faber had been commissioned to respond to the 150th anniversary of the death of Charles Dickens. The process towards publication stretched – with some extremely long gaps – over no less than 35 years. Though it is a playful story, its creation is connected to the story of Faber's grief, also his new relationship.

In the 1980s, Faber started writing a book for children called *Woman with Long-Tailed Lloriphole*, then abandoned it. After Eva's death, while touring *The Book of Strange New Things*, he read poems from what would become *Undying* as part of those events. At one literary festival, Faber met the author Louisa Young, who was in the audience. A noted Costa-shortlisted fiction writer in her own right, author of the *My Dear, I Wanted to Tell You* trilogy, she was also writing a memoir for her husband Robert, who died suddenly in 2012, called *You Left Early* (later published by Borough Press in 2018). In the following years, the two writers developed a close relationship, which started out as a shared experience of grief.

After the publication of *Undying*, Faber relocated to Kent, preferring to leave behind the Highland home he and Eva had lived in since 1999. Around this time, he read what he called 'the only two salvageable bits that had any kind of life' from *Woman with Long-Tailed Lloriphole* aloud to Louisa and her daughter, Isabel, and felt he had something to start with. Soon after, he was approached by Transworld. As he told *The Guardian*: 'I'd just moved to the south of England and it was gearing up for Brexit; I fancied writing a children's book addressing issues of where we're supposedly from and how much that matters, so I went back to the only book I'd ever attempted to write for kids.'[1] The result made for both old and new territory. In a sense, Faber was doing what he had always done – in addressing a new, much younger audience, he was continuing a lifetime habit, seeking to avoid repeating himself by hopping genres, forms and readership, while staying close to his familiar emotional territory.

*D* was an experiment in tone as well, being a much lighter read. And yet Faber readers would recognize much here. Again, a young female protagonist with no parents passing through impossible worlds in search of something almost out of reach. Again, an outsider taken from their homeland, as Faber himself was as a child. *D* is the story of an earnest 13-year-old black girl called Dhikilo from Somaliland, adopted by a couple in a small, mostly white English town. Dhikilo is morally minded and fair, taking racial micro-aggressions from those around her (who assume wrongly that she is mispronouncing the name of her homeland) in her stride.[2] Always trying to do right by those around her, she has, despite their evident racial, gender and age differences, much in common with Peter from *The Book of Strange New Things* – certainly, they both share a love of language. Indeed, as Bible language charges that novel, the alphabet itself charges *D*, Dhikilo noticing that the letter 'D' has vanished from her world. Ds disappear from the mouths of others, from road signs, from everywhere. She sets off on a fantastic voyage to return it, believing language 'wasn't just a code to communicate with: it was magic' (D 14).

*D* was initially conceived of as an illustrated book for young children, though it was published as an unillustrated, though ornate, book for young adults. (Faber is also an illustrator; he sketched illustrations for *The Crimson Petal* 20 years before.) The reasons for this change were about the children's book market, it being notoriously difficult to break into for writers of adult fiction. (Especially, perhaps, for those unlikely to keep writing books for children after this one.) Faber resisted this move, before accepting it.

In terms of the content, there was complication here, too. He wanted to write an exciting adventure story with a non-white protagonist – when it was suggested that he take out the racism protagonist Dhikilo comes across in the land of Gampalonia, the author refused, thinking it essential. He also resisted the advice of a 'sensitivity reader', believing there was an element of white readers second-guessing what readers of colour might find offensive. He took advice instead from writer and curator Sagal Farah (born in Mogadishu, Somalia),[3] English novelist Nadifa Mohamed[4] (born in Hargeisa, now part of the Republic of Somaliland), the interpreter Yurub Farah, each credited in the acknowledgements, and from Mohamed Warsame Boss, who worked at the Somaliland Mission (this is the de facto Somaliland embassy – though it cannot be called that, as the country is not recognized).[5] A more sustained study of Faber's approach to representing the life of a young black African girl would be valuable; but for now, it is clear that Faber approaches Dhikilo very much as he approached Isserley, Sugar, Peter and the Fahrenheit twins: with compassion, understanding, looking to bridge the impossible gulf, while acknowledging the gulf's existence. As the narrator says in an early chapter titled 'So Let Me Try to Help You', which includes an appeal to readers over how to address Dhikilo, 'Respect never hurts' (D 31).

So Faber attempted to pull off his usual trick; only this time, his tale of outsiderdom was transposed for a younger audience, with innocence brought to the fore, the story seen through Dhikilo's eyes. Among others, the *Washington Post* review by Ron Charles noted this link:

> There has always been an element of innocence in Faber's work, though it has often felt overwhelmed by horror and suffering. Now, though, he has made good on his vow to give up writing for adults and published *D: A Tale of Two Worlds*, which gives full voice to his gentle wit and mischievous spirit. With its buoyant sense of wonder, *D* is a novel graciously indebted to the fantasies of C. S. Lewis, James Thurber and Norton Juster, along with the characters of Charles Dickens. The result is a rare book that mature readers will appreciate on one level while younger readers enjoy on another.[6]

Not all reviewers were as supportive – UK newspapers who had often lauded Faber, such as the *Telegraph* and *Guardian*, gave *D* a mixed response. But the jacket of the US edition, replete with Neil Gaiman endorsement and magical, sparkling spyglass, showed who this book was for. Only recently published in paperback, it is perhaps too soon to fully consider the place of *D* in Faber's wider oeuvre, though commonalities are clear.

## FUTURE PROJECTS

In late 2022, Faber wrote one more email responding to my questions, in which he identified the projects he could envisage himself completing in future. The first of these is a non-fiction book about music, provisionally titled *Listen*. As we have seen, music has been a recurring feature in Faber's fiction from the beginning, while the author has claimed to listen to up to ten hours of music a day, this and his comics collection being more important to him than any fiction. Initially focusing on what he calls 'all the supposedly naff music genres: autotune pop, extreme death metal, Christian rock...'[7] before radically cutting down, turning instead to the emotional connection that listening allows lovers of music, Faber had previously joked that his deadline for his long-threatened book might be 'the year 3000' – but he has been known to disrupt expectations before. By 2022, this music book had become so big that it had to be divided into two volumes. *Listen*, the first of these, will be published in Autumn 2023, though at the time of writing its shape and focus is not yet set. Another project which has come together in fragmented, disrupted ways over a long period of time, it again stands apart from his other work in terms of genre, form and potential audience.[8]

Alongside these, there is also a pair of what we might call 'Eva books'. In interviews around the time of *Undying*, Faber talked openly about the biography of her life he was writing, for Eva's descendants only, not for publication. Six years later that book is 'currently very big and lopsided and unevenly crafted'. Faber explains his plan: 'If my own lifespan permits, I'll work on it some more. But it's not an artistic project. Whatever shape it's in when I die will be the shape it's in.'[9] Again, then, a Faber project unlike any other. As is the second Eva book, which the author has worked on in bursts since her death. This is a book of her unfinished, unpublished short stories. He aims to complete these, imitating her style. If *Undying* initially seemed like a one-off exercise in grief about an intense period of loss, this now looks more like just one part of an uncommon, sustained effort to remember Eva's life and work.

In terms of the short stories, Faber has discussed publishing these under both their names, with some mostly written by her, others mostly by him, each seeking to retain her distinct literary voice. At the time of writing, Faber has several of these ready for publication. After so many collaborations, here is his attempt to collaborate with Eva, in her absence. Again highly unusual, this project is also typical of Faber's lifelong approach. Many writers would consider a man attempting to 'complete' his dead wife's stories to be impossibly thorny territory. Faber disagrees.

Meanwhile, he also envisages an uncommon book of photographs accompanied with short written texts. The photos are of the doll he carries with him wherever he goes, called 'The Intrepid Blonde', a curious but typically Faber-esque creation he has photographed around the world, taking a keen interest in whatever she finds, a blend of the innocent and the strangely sinister. The book will be based on an Instagram account. 'The IB' hiding under a plant. Using a gin glass as a 'beautiful crystal font for washing her hands in'.[10] Gazing up at open-air karaoke lyrics. (Unsurprisingly, Faber himself is not on social media. Though Louisa is.) As this last project in particular makes clear, these artistic decisions are not made with a writer's 'career' or 'audience' in mind. Singular of mind as ever, solitary, certain of his own path. He carries on.

Aside from the above, what else? Interestingly, Faber considers another collection of short stories possible. This seems likely, given the large amount of material still unpublished, also his habit of returning to old work. Faber points to 'Bye Bye Natalia', which just missed the cut for *The Fahrenheit Twins* in 2005, as one he would like to revisit. He does not believe he has 'enough sufficiently strong stories for a full collection' yet,[11] though recent story 'The Morning After' might qualify, having just been published in Scottish literary magazine *Extra Teeth* in 2023. Of all these projects mentioned, this one seems most like an aspiration, rather than a statement of intent. As Faber puts it himself: 'Good new stories will happen if they happen.' Well, he has always been a writer of stories.

Whatever happens, it seems likely that Michel Faber will keep approaching projects as he always has. With a healthy disrespect for conventional publishing wisdom, a singular vision and a powerful instinct for compassion on the page, no matter what.

# Notes

## CHAPTER 1: FABER'S WORLD OF THE SHORT STORY

1. MF interview with Justine Jordan, *The Guardian*, 8/7/16.
2. MF email to RG, 18/2/21.
3. MF email to RG, 3/2/22.
4. Ibid.
5. Interview with Thomas Oberender, 'Michel Faber: Transnational and Transplanetary Literature', SAND, 2019, https://sandjournal.com/michel-faber/.
6. Dundee Archives MS 334/069.
7. Ibid.
8. Ibid.
9. MF email to RG, 28/2/22: 'A couple of "nursing" short stories... are TOTALLY autobiographical': 'She Spells It Out to Me with Two Fingers', *Edinburgh Review* (1992) and 'Me and My First Wife', re-titled 'Hole' (unpublished).
10. MF email to RG, 19/2/21.
11. Interview with Justine Jordan, *The Guardian*, 8/7/16.
12. MF email to RG, 20/8/21.
13. Dundee Archives MS 334/069.
14. Interview with Justine Jordan, *The Guardian*, 8/7/16.
15. MF email to RG, 28/2/22.
16. Ibid.
17. Dundee Archives MS 334/069.
18. JM email to RG, 4/3/22.
19. Dundee Archives MS 334/069.
20. JM email to RG, 4/3/22.
21. Ibid.
22. MF email to RG, 20/8/21.
23. Ibid.

24 Sue Zlosnik, 'Globalgothic at the Top of the World: Michel Faber's "The Fahrenheit Twins"', in Glennis Byron (ed.): *Globalgothic* (Manchester University Press, 2013), p. 66.
25 When asked to clarify if he'd read Munro, MF replied: 'I'm not sure. Eva really liked her. So it's possible Munro is one of those authors I read a few pages of, or a chapter or a short story, so that Eva & I could have a fun hour discussing the techniques, how they differed from other authors... One thing is 100% sure – Munro is not an influence.' Email to RG, 3/9/22.
26 Ailsa Cox, *Alice Munro* (Northcote House, 2003), p. 7.
27 Ibid., p. 8.
28 M. John Harrison. 'The Future Tense', *The Guardian*, 3/9/05, https://www.theguardian.com/books/2005/sep/03/featuresreviews.guardianreview13.

## CHAPTER 2: FABER'S WORLD OF THE NOVELLA (OR MEDIUM-SIZED STORY)

1 Ian McEwan, 'Notes on the Novella', *The New Yorker*, 29/10/12 https://www.newyorker.com/books/page-turner/some-notes-on-the-novella.
2 RG interview with JM, 8/4/22.
3 These were not included in subsequent editions.
4 'Part historical thriller, part gothic romance, part ghost story, it is further confirmation that its author is a singular talent with a unique perception of the universe.' *Sunday Herald*, 2001.
5 As described by MF, email to RG, 14/9/22: '[T]he problem is eventually revealed to be gravel from her Bosnia accident which has been slowly working its way to the surface.'
6 MF email to RG, 7/4/22: 'I think both *The Hundred and Ninety-Nine Steps* and *The Courage Consort* functioned partly as "safety valves" in that I was writing them during the rewriting/overhauling of *Petal* which was such a huge project to hold in my head that I occasionally needed to focus on something else for a while. I'd actually been hatching *The Courage Consort* since the mid-1980s when I heard a long radio interview with Terry Edwards, the baritone of Electric Phoenix. It was just a matter of finding the right story.'
7 MF interview with Jill Adams, *Barcelona Review*, 2002, https://barcelonareview.com/29/e_mf_int.htm.
8 MF email to RG, 24/3/22, alongside photo of thumbnail sketches for TCC.
9 MF interview with Jill Adams, *Barcelona Review*, 2002, https:/barcelonareview.com/29/e_mf_int.htm.

NOTES

10 Jamie Jauncey, 'The Courage Consort: Striking a new kind of Dischord', *The Scotsman*, 19/1/22, p. 10.
11 MF, notes on JM's email to RG, 5/3/22.
12 MF had previously sent 1996 story 'Do You Mind if We Videotape This?', due to be in the third anthology in the critically acclaimed Scottish series starting with *The Children of Albion Rovers*, to Rebel Inc. magazine's editor Kevin Williamson in 1997. Unknown to the author, the Rebel Inc. PO box had been closed in 1995 along with the magazine (KW email to RG, 2/2/22).
13 MF's email to RG, 4/3/22, explains how this was a contributing factor in changing Byng's opinion of 'The Fahrenheit Twins'.
14 Fahrenheit Twins released two albums in the early 2010s, most recently *Breekpunt* (2014), a soundtrack to the Dutch indie film of the same name: https://fahrenheittwins.bandcamp.com/ (accessed 5/3/22).
15 Sue Zlosnik, 'Globalgothic at the Top of the World: Michel Faber's "The Fahrenheit Twins"', in Glennis Byron (ed.): *Globalgothic* (Manchester University Press, 2013), p. 67.
16 Ibid.

**CHAPTER 3: FABER'S WORLD OF THE NOVEL**

1 MF email to RG, 14/9/22: 'The MS was at one point given to Stephanie Wolfe-Murray of Canongate to read, as she had said it sounded the most interesting of the unpublished novels I'd described to her. She lost it and it was never read.'
2 MF email to RG, 8/2/22.
3 MF email to RG, 25/2/22.
4 Ibid.
5 MF email to RG, 8/2/22.
6 Interview with Justine Jordan, *The Guardian*, 8/7/16.
7 Interview with Thomas Oberender, 'Michel Faber: Transnational and Transplanetary Literature', SAND, 2019, https://sandjournal.com/michel-faber/.
8 This was explored in 'The Perfect W', the story Moir lamented not making the cut for *Some Rain Must Fall*.
9 Faber, 'Under the Skin changed my life for good', *The Guardian*, 5/12/20, https://www.theguardian.com/books/2020/dec/05/michel-faber-under-the-skin-changed-my-life-for-good.
10 MF email to RG, 24/3/22: 'I imagined Isserley's original form (before her reconstructive surgery) to be a sort of combination of the woman in the photo and the llamas.'

11 Ibid.
12 Dundee Archives MS 334/069.
13 Ibid.
14 This option was held from 2000 to 2003, then dropped. In 2003, rights were bought by Jonathan Glazer, director of the 2013 film version.
15 Ibid.
16 JM interview with RG, 8/4/22.
17 MF email to RG, 24/3/22.
18 Ibid.
19 Interview with Thomas Oberender, 'Michel Faber: Transnational and Transplanetary Literature', SAND, 2019, https://sandjournal.com/michel-faber/.
20 *Not One More Death* (Verso, 2006).
21 Ibid., p. 52.
22 Interview with Justine Jordan, *The Guardian*, 8/7/16.
23 *The Skinny*, interview with Michel Faber, 2014, https://www.theskinny.co.uk/books/features/unto-the-end-michel-faber-on-his-last-masterpiece.
24 Ibid.
25 MF email to RG, 7/4/22.
26 MF email to RG, 7/4/22.
27 MF email to RG, 3/2/22.
28 Faber readers may recognize the phrase 'strange new things' from that early short story Judy Moir so loved, 'Toy Story', in which God was reaching out, impossibly distant from his people.
29 MF email to RG, 7/4/22.

## CHAPTER 4: FABER'S WORLD OF *THE CRIMSON PETAL*

1 From 'Eccentricity and Authenticity: Fact into Fiction', an essay by MF which appeared in Volume 31 (2003) of *Victorians Institute Journal*, the sixth of a group of seven short pieces designated a special feature, 'Ghosts of the Victorian'.
2 Ibid.
3 For example, under Emmeline Fox, MF wrote longhand: 'loves Henry Rackham – dying (of consumption, I suppose)', MF's personal home archive, dramatis personae for TCP, 1979.
4 MF and Eva Faber joint interview, *The List*, 24/3/11, https://list.co.uk/news/23901/michel-faber-interview-the-crimson-petal-and-the-white (accessed 14/2/22).
5 Interview with Thomas Oberender, 'Michel Faber: Transnational and Transplanetary Literature', SAND, 2019, https://sandjournal.com/michel-faber/.

NOTES

6 Canongate's history: https://canongate.co.uk/about/.
7 RG interview with JM, 8/4/22
8 MF letter to JM (undated), Dundee Archives MS 334/069.
9 MF letter to JM, 15/3/00, Dundee Archives MS 334/069.
10 MF letter to Fielding, 9/5/00.
11 RC letter to MF, 14/11/00.
12 MF and Eva Youren joint interview, *The List*, 24/3/11, https://list.co.uk/news/23901/michel-faber-interview-the-crimson-petal-and-the-white (accessed 14/2/22).
13 MF letter to JM, 11/12/01, Dundee Archives MS 334/069.
14 MF letter to JM, 27/1/02, Dundee Archives MS 334/069. Antoni Libera's 1998 novel *Madame* was nominated for the 2002 Dublin IMPAC Award, alongside *Under the Skin*.
15 James R. Kincaid, review of TCP, 'The Nanny Diaries', *New York Times*, 15/9/02. Clipping found in Dundee Archives MS 334/069.
16 Faber also quoted Tennyson in the epigraph to *The Hundred and Ninety-Nine Steps*.
17 BookBrowse interview with MF, 2002, https://www.bookbrowse.com/author_interviews/full/index.cfm/author_number/822/Michel-Faber.
18 James R. Kincaid, review of TCP, 'The Nanny Diaries', *New York Times*, 15/9/02. Clipping found in Dundee Archives MS 334/069.
19 Ibid.
20 Ibid.
21 BookBrowse interview with MF, 2002, https://www.bookbrowse.com/author_interviews/full/index.cfm/author_number/822/Michel-Faber.
22 Kathryn Hughes, 'Whores, Porn and Lunatics', *The Guardian*, 28/9/02, https://www.theguardian.com/books/2002/sep/28/fiction.
23 Clipping from *Time* magazine, found in Dundee Archives MS 334/069.

## CHAPTER 5: FABER'S WORLD OF VERSE

1 MF interview with Justine Jordan, *The Guardian*, 8/7/16.
2 MF email to RG, 14/9/22.
3 Allan Massie, 'Book review: Undying, A Love Story by Michael [sic] Faber', *The Scotsman*, 9/7/16, https://www.scotsman.com/arts-and-culture/books/book-review-undying-love-story-michael-faber-1472526# (accessed 5/2/22). (A later web version of the review credited the reviewer, Allan Massie, by name.)
4 Ibid.
5 Scottish Poetry Library, https://www.scottishpoetrylibrary.org.uk/poem/dont-hesitate-ask/.

6 Ibid.
7 Allan Massie, 'Book review: Undying, A Love Story by Michael [sic] Faber', *The Scotsman*, 9/7/16, https://www.scotsman.com/arts-and-culture/books/book-review-undying-love-story-michael-faber-1472526# (accessed 5/2/22).
8 MF interview with Justine Jordan, *The Guardian*, 8/7/16.
9 MF email to RG, 14/9/22: 'There will never be another poetry collection.'

## CHAPTER 6: FABER, OUT OF TIME

1 Michel Faber, 'I don't read fiction any more', *The Guardian*, 5/9/20, https://www.theguardian.com/books/2020/sep/05/michel-faber-i-dont-read-fiction-any-more (accessed 19/5/22).
2 MF email to RG, 17/9/22: 'Overall, Somaliland has had a much more peaceful and stable existence than Somalia. This is one of the reasons why the Somalilanders are so frustrated with the world's refusal to recognise them as a country. Somaliland would make a much safer bet for foreign investment than Somalia.'
3 Profile at Dutch Art Institute, https://dutchartinstitute.eu/page/16453/sagal-farah (accessed 13/9/22).
4 Profile at British Council Literature, https://literature.britishcouncil.org/writer/nadifa-mohamed (accessed 13/9/22).
5 http://www.somaliland-mission.com/ (accessed 17/9/22).
6 Ron Charles, 'Michel Faber's *D* is a quirky adventure for readers young and old', *The Washington Post*, 14/12/20, https://www.washingtonpost.com/entertainment/books/d-michel-faber-book-review/2020/12/14/7e707762-3d99-11eb-8bc0-ae155bee4aff_story.html.
7 Michel Faber, 'I don't read fiction any more', *The Guardian*, 5/9/20, https://www.theguardian.com/books/2020/sep/05/michel-faber-i-dont-read-fiction-any-more (accessed 19/5/22).
8 MF email to RG, 17/5/22: 'For various reasons, including the vastness of the project, the unfeasibly large amount of stuff I've already written, and the unfortunate way Covid has hampered the interviews with foreign musicians that I'd hoped to be able to do, the project has been divided into two books. The first of them is scheduled for publication in 2023.'
9 Ibid.
10 The IB with gin glass, https://www.instagram.com/p/CZO73w8s2TN/ (accessed 21/5/22).
11 MF email to RG, 17/5/22: 'The other two stories I've written in the last couple of years were commissions for Italian magazines and very specific to their intended readership.'

# Select Bibliography

**Fiction by Michel Faber**

'Adopt a Tiger', *Big Issue Australia*, date unknown
*The Apple: Crimson Petal Stories* (Canongate, 2006). Contains: 'Foreword'; 'Christmas in Silver Street'; 'Clara and the Rat Man'; 'Chocolate Hearts from the New World'; 'The Fly, and its Effect on Mr Bodley'; 'The Apple'; 'Medicine'; 'A Mighty Horde of Women in Very Big Hats, Advancing'
'Bed & Breakfast', *The Erotic Review*, date unknown
*The Book of Strange New Things* (Canongate, 2014)
*The Courage Consort* (Canongate, 2001)
*The Crimson Petal and the White* (Canongate, 2002)
*D: A Tale of Two Worlds* (Transworld, 2020)
*The Hundred and Ninety-Nine Steps* (Canongate, 2001)
*The Fahrenheit Twins* (Canongate, 2005). Contains: 'The Safehouse'; 'Andy Comes Back'; 'The Eyes of the Soul'; 'Serious Swimmers'; 'Explaining Coconuts'; 'Finesse'; 'Flesh Remains Flesh'; 'Less Than Perfect'; 'A Hole With Two Ends'; 'The Smallness of the Action'; 'All Black'; 'Mouse'; 'Someone to Kiss it Better'; 'Beyond Pain'; 'Tabitha Warren'; 'Vanilla-Bright like Eminem'; 'The Fahrenheit Twins'
*The Fire Gospel* (Canongate, 2008)
'The Morning After', *Extra Teeth* magazine, issue 7 (forthcoming, 2023)
'She Spells It Out to Me with Two Fingers', *Edinburgh Review*, 1992
*Some Rain Must Fall* (Canongate, 1998). Contains: 'Some Rain Must Fall'; 'Fish'; 'In Case of Vertigo'; 'Toy Story'; 'Miss Fatt and Miss Thinne'; 'Half a Million Pounds and a Miracle'; 'The Red Cement Truck'; 'Somewhere Warm and Comfortable'; 'Nina's Hand'; 'The Crust of Hell'; 'The Gossip Cell'; 'Accountability'; 'Pidgin American'; 'The Tunnel of Love'; 'Sheep'
*Under the Skin* (Canongate, 2000)

## Poetry by Michel Faber

*Undying: A Love Story* (Canongate, 2014)

## Faber in Anthologies and Online

'The Broccoli Eel', published in *The Guardian*, 2/8/2003, https://www.theguardian.com/books/2003/aug/02/originalwriting.fiction7 (accessed 14/2/23)
'Bye Bye Natalia', short story published in *Granta 94: On The Road Again* (Granta, 2006)
'Depth of Field', published in *Groundswell* (date unknown)
'A Flash of Blue Light', short story in *Elsewhere: Somewhere* (Cargo/McSweeney's, 2012)
'A Hole with Two Ends', in Alan Bissett (ed.): *Damage Land: New Scottish Gothic Fiction* (Polygon, 2001)
'Missing Photographs', published in *New Scottish Writing* (Flamingo/HarperCollins, 1997)
'Walking After Midnight', in *Ox-Tales: Water* (Profile, 2009) – chapter from then-forthcoming *The Book of Strange New Things*

## Faber Essays

'Dreams in the Dumpster, Language Down the Drain', in *Not One More Death* (Verso, 2006)
'Eccentricity and Authenticity: Fact into Fiction', *Victorians Institute Journal*, Volume 31 (2003), pp. 100–103

## Unpublished Faber Resources

'The Collar' (short story)
'Down the Up Escalator in the Race Against Science' (short story)
Email correspondence between MF and RG, 2020–2022
'The Highland Clearances' (short story)
'Hole' (originally titled 'Me and My First Wife')
Michel Faber's personal short-story database (accessed by permission of the author for the purposes of this book)
'The Perfect W' (short story)
*A Photograph of Jesus* (novel, 1987)
'Taking Care of Big Brother' (broadcast on BBC Radio 4, 1999)

## Music

'Steam Comes off Our House', by De Rosa (lyrics written by Michel Faber, from album *Ballads of the Book*, Chemikal Underground, 2007)

## Selected Interviews

Interview with Thomas Oberender, Internationales Literaturfestival Berlin 2019, as published in SAND Journal, 'Michel Faber: Transnational and Transplanetary Literature', www.sandjournal.com/michel-faber/ (published 26/3/2020)

Michel Faber and David Mitchell joint interview: 'Two of this generation's best novelists of life, love and literature', *The Independent*, 22/11/14, https://www.independent.co.uk/arts-entertainment/books/features/david-mitchell-and-michel-faber-interview-two-of-this-generation-s-best-novelists-on-love-life-and-literature-9875894.html (accessed 13/9/22)

Michel and Eva Faber interview: 'Michel Faber Interview: The Crimson Petal and the White' by Claire Sawers, *The List*, 24/3/11, https://list.co.uk/news/23901/michel-faber-interview-the-crimson-petal-and-the-white (accessed 14/2/22)

'Michel Faber: This is my last novel', *The Bookseller*, 23/10/14, https://www.thebookseller.com/news/michel-faber-my-last-novel (accessed 13/9/22)

## Selected Critical Work on Faber

Dillon, Sarah (2011), '"It's a Question of Words, Therefore": Becoming Animal in Michel Faber's *Under the Skin*', *Science Fiction Studies* 38 (1), pp. 134–154

Langworthy, Rebecca, Lindfield-Ott, Kristin and MacPherson, Jim (eds.), *Michel Faber: Critical Essays* (Gylphi Contemporary Writers Series, 2020)

Lindfield-Ott, Kristin (2016), 'Fear in Fearn: Place and Imagination in Michel Faber's Ross-shire Fiction', *Northern Scotland* 7, pp. 64–84

Llewellyn, Mark (2012), 'Authenticity, Authority and the Author: The Sugared Voice of the Neo-Victorian in *The Crimson Petal and the White*', in Claire Westall and Rina Kim (eds.): *Cross-Gendered Literary Voices: Appropriating, Resisting, Embracing* (Palgrave Macmillan), pp. 185–203

Zlosnik, Sue (2013), 'Globalgothic at the Top of the World: Michel Faber's "The Fahrenheit Twins"', in Glennis Byron (ed.): *Globalgothic* (Manchester University Press), pp. 65–76

# Index

10.18 (French publisher) 14

Abbess Hild 34
Ablach Farm 63–67
absence 51, 53
abuse 26, 86, 93, 97–98
accuracy 81, 83–84
affection 37
Afghanistan xiii, 70
Aldgate 84
alienation 2, 8, 25, 57–58
aliens 68, 70, 71, 76, 87, 111
Amazon 70
ambition 8, 9
*American Psycho* 55
anachronism 81
Anderson, Gillian xiii, 95
antagonist, lack of 79
Arctic 45–47, 51
Arthur C. Clarke Award 69
Atwood, Margaret 69
Australia ix, 7, 8, 55, 83
autobiographical writing 4, 8, 9, 62, 105

Baker, Timothy B. 15–16
Ballads of the Book xiii
Bayswater High xi
BBC
   mini-series, *Crimson Petal* 95
   Radio 4 xii
   Radio Scotland xii
   TV xiii

Belgium 40–41, 46
Bergman, Ingrid 63
Bickmore, Francis
*Big Issue Australia, The* 44
birds 16
body issues 58
Bogart, Humphrey 63
Book of Knowledge 4, 7
Booker Prize 82
*Bookseller, The* 61
Boronia High School xi
Bosnia 34
Boss, Mohamed Warsame 115
boundaries 2, 15, 16, 33, 49
Boycott, Rosie 83
Brexit 114
Brown, Jenny 13
Buchan, John 34
Byatt, A.S. 69
Byng, Jamie 9, 13, 44–45, 61, 69, 82–83

cancer xiii, xiv, 4, 35, 53, 68, 70, 72, 105–112 (see also Youren, Eva)
cannibalism 98
Canongate xii, 4, 13, 55, 60, 69, 71, 82, 110
   The Myths series xiii, 32, 69
   writer–publisher relationship 14
categorization 1
certainty, undermining of 29–30

129

# INDEX

characterization 25, 43, 54, 84
Charles, Ron 116
Chemikal Underground xiii
children's literature 114, 116 (see also Faber, Michel, books, *D: A Tale of Two Worlds*)
Christianity 73–79, 84, 90, 92, 101, 104
Christmas 93
chronology 1
Cline, Roger 84
closure 99, 102–103
*Cloud Atlas* 58
comedy 86
commercial success 3, 39, 40, 69, 83, 99
communication 18–19, 47–48, 77, 79
compassion 2, 3, 42, 53–55, 58–59, 68, 77–78, 101, 115, 118
competitions 12 (see also Macallan Short Story Award; Neil M. Gunn Award; St James Story Award; Saltire Society Book of the Year; Saltire Society First Book of the Year)
confidence 11, 42, 54, 60–62
connection
  impossibility of, lack of 21, 24–25, 50–51, 58, 109
  search for 15, 20, 33, 42, 47–48, 57, 74–75, 77–78, 116
consumerism 55
cosmetic surgery 13–14, 59
Cox, Ailsa 27
creative process 1, 3, 59, 68, 72, 82, 112
creative writing 4
*Crimson Petal and the White, The* (TV series) xiii (see also Faber, Michel, books, *Crimson Petal and the White, The*)
critical acclaim 14, 25, 69, 111
culture 1

*Daily Mail* 39, 111
*Daily Telegraph* 39, 116
Davidson, Toni 14
Dawkins, Richard 70
depression 11, 40
Dewhurst, Emily 13
Dickens, Charles 96, 114, 116
Dignitas 108
dignity 110
distance 74–75
Dodson, Betty PhD 85
Dublin IMPAC Award xii, xiv, 85
Dutch Baptists 7
Dutch characters 40

Edinburgh 13
Edinburgh International Book Festival xiii
editorial 3, 12
Eichborn (German publisher) 14
Einaudi (Italian publisher) 14
Electric Phoenix a cappella ensemble (Terry Phoenix) 38
Ellis, Bret Easton 55
emotional effect 59, 71–73
emotional territory 15, 59, 115
empathy 18–19, 96
England 1
English Heritage 33
environmental catastrophe 76–77
environmental writing 33
epistolary writing 19–21, 26, 34, 75, 94
*Erotic Review, The* 44
*Evening Standard* 34
experimentation 11
extreme settings 11, 47, 51

Faber, Michel
  family of 7, 8
  father of 7
  mother of 7
  teenager, Faber as 1, 7, 8, 54, 97, 105

130

anthologies containing work
by
*Elsewhere* xiii
*Not One More Death* xiii, 70
*Ox-Tales: Water* xiii
books
   *The Apple: Crimson Petal Stories* xiii, 2, 3, 69, 81, 85, 99–104
      Agnes Rackham 99–100
      Henry Rackham (senior) 100–101, 104
      Henry Rackham (junior, son of Sophie Rackham in 'A Mighty Horde...') 101–103
      Sophie Rackham 99–101, 103
      William Rackham 99–103
   *Book of Strange New Things, The* xiii, xiv, 1, 3, 47, 53, 56, 67–79, 87, 106, 113–115
      invented language 71, 74
      narrative of 73–77
      Oasans 68, 71, 73, 75–79
      Oasis xiv, 68–69, 72, 74–76, 78
      Peter 74–80, 115
      writing of 69, 71, 78
   *Courage Consort, The* xii, 3, 32, 38–42, 85, 111
      Catherine, character of 40–43
      narrative of 40–42
      reception to 39–40, 42
   *Crimson Petal and the White, The* xi, xii, 1, 2, 3, 38, 39, 44–45, 55, 70, 81–89, 99–103, 113, 115
      Agnes Rackham 91, 86, 89–95, 97–98
      book jacket of 85
      Church Lane 88, 92, 95
      Henry Rackham (character, writing of) 84–86, 90, 92–93
      narrative of 86–90
      reception pf 83, 95
      research for 9, 33, 53, 83–84
      resistance to sequel for 81, 99, 102–103
      Sophie Rackham 87, 90, 92–95, 98
      Sugar 82, 84, 86–95, 97–103, 116
      William Rackham 82, 84–95, 97–98
      writing of, editorial for 82–85
   *D: A Tale of Two Worlds* xiv, 1, 113–116
      Dhikilo 115–116
      earlier version, *Woman with Long-Tailed Lloriphole* 114
      reception to 115–117
      Somaliland 115–116
   *Fahrenheit Twins, The* xiii, 3, 25–30, 69
      reception to 25, 30
   *Fire Gospel, The* xiii, 32, 47, 53, 56–57, 69–70
      narrative summary 69–70
   *Hundred and Ninety-Nine Steps, The* xii, 3, 32, 33–39, 40, 42, 49, 85
      narrative of 34–35
      reception to 33, 38, 42
      research for 33
      Siân, character of 34–37, 40, 42
   *Listen* xiv, 117
   *Photograph of Jesus, A* xi, 1, 3, 53–58, 60, 69–70
      narrative overview of 54–55
      New Wave Christians 55, 57

# INDEX

*Some Rain Must Fall* xii, 3, 60–61
  critical assessment of 15
  foreign rights sales 14
  preparation of 13, 44
  reception 14
*Three Novellas* 32, 45, 69
*Under the Skin* (see also *Under the Skin*, film) xii, 3, 39, 44, 53, 58–70, 74, 76, 87, 111
  hitchhikers 61, 63–67, 111
  invented language 64–67
  Isserley 58, 60–68, 87, 116
  narrative of 59, 64–68
  writing of, editorial process 14, 61–63
*Undying: A Love Story* xiv, 3, 105–112, 117
  reception of 110
  structure of 105–110
*Vanilla Bright like Eminem* xiii, 25 (see also individual stories, 'The Fahrenheit Twins')
  reception of 26
individual poems
  'Cowboys' 106
  'Don't Hesitate to Ask' 109
  'Helpmeet' 108
  '(indecipherable) kappa' 108
  'Lucky' 107
  'Nipples' 106
  'Of Old Age, In Our Sleep' xi, 105
  'Old Bird, Not Very Well' xii, 106
  'Old People in Hospital' xi, 106
  'Our Cats No Longer Miss You' 109
  'Switzerland' 108
  'Your Plants' 109

individual stories
  'Accountability' 20
  'Adopt a Tiger' 44
  'A Flash of Blue Light' xiii
  'A Mighty Horde of Women in Very Big Hats, Advancing' 2, 100–103
  'A Million Pounds and a Miracle' 12–13
  'Bed & Breakfast' 44
  'Bye Bye Natalia' xiii
  'Chocolate Hearts from the New World' xiii, 101
  'Christmas in Silver Street' xii, 99
  'Clara and the Rat Man' 100–101, 103
  'Down the Up Escalator in a Race Against Science' (unpublished) 12
  'Dreams in the Dumpster, Language Down the Drain' xiii
  'Fish' xi, xii, 3, 10, 12, 16, 22–24, 49
    narrative of 22–23
  'Half a Million Pounds and a Miracle' xii
  'In Case of Vertigo' 17
  'Knabbel and Babbel Go to the Moon' xi
  'Me and My First Wife' (later retitled 'Hole') 44
  'Medicine' 100, 103
  'Miss Fatt and Miss Thinne' 10, 17
  'Nina's Hand' 18, 100
  'Pidgin American' 18
  'Serious Swimmers' 30
  'She Spells It Out to Me with Two Fingers' 119
  'Sheep' 11, 16
  'Some Rain Must Fall' xii, 3, 12, 16, 21–22
    narrative of 19–20

# INDEX

'Somewhere Warm and Comfortable' 17–18, 100
'Tabitha Warren' 20, 26, 30
'Taking Care of Big Brother' xii, 39
'Toy Story' 12, 16–17, 101
'The Apple' 100–101
'The Broccoli Eel' 44
'The Collar' (unpublished) 12
'The Crust of Hell' 11
'The Eyes of the Soul' 26
'The Fahrenheit Twins' 3, 11, 26, 44–51, 53
  Boris Fahrenheit, betrayal of 49–50
  Dutch band of the same name 45
  Miss Kristensen, arrival of 50–51
  narrative of 45–46
  Told by an Idiot theatre production 45
  Una Fahrenheit, death of 49
  Una Fahrenheit, ritual burial of 49
'The Fly, and its Effect on Mr Bodley' 100
'The Highland Clearances' (unpublished) 12
'The Perfect W' (unpublished) 13
'The Safehouse' xiii, 10, 20, 26, 30, 44
'The Smallness of the Action' 30
'The Tunnel of Love' 18
'Vanilla-Bright like Eminem' (short story; see also books, *Vanilla Bright like Eminem*) 3, 26–30
'Walking After Midnight' (see also books, *Book of Strange New Things, The*) xiii

collaborations with
  Brian Eno podcast version of 'The Fahrenheit Twins' with music 45
  De Rosa, 'Steam Comes off Our House' xiii
works about
  *Michel Faber: Critical Essays* xiv, 4
Faber protagonists 20
Faber Studies 4
faith 36, 53–57, 66–71, 73, 75, 77–79
fantastic, the 3, 10, 22, 34, 87, 109, 114–115
fantasy (secondary world) 48
Farah, Sagal 115
Farah, Yurub 115
Fearn Station House xii, 110
feminism, feminist writing 90, 100–101
Fielding, Dr Kenneth (University of Edinburgh) 83–84
flashbacks 22
Foley, Matt 98
form 1
fractal structure 64
fragility 30, 41, 63, 71, 90, 106
*Frankenstein* 45
Frankfurt Book Fair 14
future projects 117–118
  biography of Eva, for her family (not for publication) 117
  Intrepid Blonde photograph book 117
  short stories project, with Eva Faber 117

Gaiman, Neil 116
Galloway, Janice 69
*Game of Thrones* 69
Garai, Romola xiii, 95
gender assumptions 78
gender politics 58

133

genre 1, 19, 59, 66, 105, 117
Gerrard, Grayson xi
  emigration with 9
  marriage to 9
Glazer, Jonathan xiii, 59
God 17, 47, 89–90, 109
Gothic, the 33–34, 46
Grant, Richard E. 95
Gray, Alasdair 39
grief 94, 105, 107, 108–111, 114, 117
Grossman, David 69
Grossman, Lev 97
*Guardian, The* 38, 39, 42, 44, 111, 114, 116
Guhiynui 46, 49–50
guilt 7, 67, 72, 108
gulfs 15–16, 19–20, 28, 110, 116
*Gulliver's Travels* 63

Hague, The xi
Hansel and Gretel 46
happiness 29
Harcourt Brace (US publisher) 14, 45, 61
Hardy, Thomas 111
Harrison, M. John 30
Hatoum, Milton 69
haunting 34
historical fiction 1, 34, 39, 100
homelessness 10
horror 1, 7, 51, 55, 59, 86, 108, 112, 116
hospitals xiv
Hughes, Kathryn 96
hybridization, hybridity 1, 2, 14, 59, 105

idealization 91, 100
identity 63
illness 4, 72
illustration 8, 115
implausibility 63
impulsiveness 65, 67
internality 23, 97
Iraq xiii, 69–70

Jack the Ripper 84
Jackson Young, David 39
*Jane Eyre* 96
Jauncey, Jamie 42
Johansson, Scarlett xiii, 59
Jordan, Justine 42, 111–112
Juster, Norton 116

Kelman, James 39
Kennedy, A.L. 39
Kent 114
Kincaid, James R. 96
King James Bible 73

language 2, 97, 115
*Last Exit to Leith* 44
le Carré, John 70
Le Seuil 61
Levi, Mica xiii
Lewis, C.S. 7, 116
Libere, Antoni 85
*Life of Pi* 82
literary fiction 9
llamas 60
Lockerbie, Catherine 109
London xiii, xiv, 10, 18, 36, 45, 62, 83, 85–87, 90, 103, 106
London Topographical Society 84
loneliness 12, 17, 34, 55
loss 25
love 53, 71, 75, 110

Macallan Short Story Award xii, 12, 13
*Madame* 85
Madden, Richard 69
Marko'cain and Tainto'lilith 45–51
Martel, Yann 92
Massie, Allan 111
McEwan, Ian 31, 110
McSweeney's xiii
medium-sized stories 2, 3, 44, 100

# INDEX

Melbourne xi, 7
  move to 8
  University of xi, 81
menstruation 91
micro-aggressions 115
migraines 10
*mise-en-scène* 76
misunderstanding 16, 18 (see also communication)
Mitchell, David 58
Mohamed, Nadifah 115
Moir, Judy 11, 12, 13, 33, 39, 45, 60–63, 83–85
Mooney, Bel 111
moral outlook, moral writing 15, 68, 86, 90, 96, 104
Munro, Alice 26–27
music 55, 113, 117
  in Faber's fiction 40, 42
  writing about xi, 8, 9, 117
*My Dear, I Wanted to Tell You* 114

National Short Story Award (later BBC National Short Story Award) xiii
nations 1
natural world 42
Nazis
  collaboration with 7
  legacy of 40
Neil M. Gunn Award xii, 12–13
Netherlands ix, 7
neurodivergence 8
*New York Times, The* 96
*Newsnight Review* 83
non-human animals 16, 33, 35, 63, 67
  Hadrian/Hush the dog 35–38
  huskies 46, 49, 50
  Joshua the cat 74, 78 (in *The Book of Strange New Things*)
  (see also Faber, Michel, books, *Under the Skin*, Isserley)
novellas 2, 3, 39
  definition of 31

novels 1, 31, 53, 57–58, 81, 99
'Now Sleeps the Crimson Petal' 86
nursing xii, 9, 11, 82, 105–106

O'Dowd, Chris xiii
O'Hagan, Andrew 69
*Oasis* (TV series pilot, Amazon Prime) xiv, 69
obsession 55–56, 91–92
*On the Road* 63
Ostrov Providenya (imagined place) 45, 48
Ostrov Provideniya (real place) 48
otherness, othering 58, 66

pace 29–30
painting 8
parent–child relationships 24–25
*Partitum Mutante* 40, 42–43
Patty, Ann 82, 99
perspective, shift of 35
physicality 65, 78
Pinter, Harold 70
Podium (Dutch publisher) 14
Poe, Edgar Allen 51
poetry 4, 105–106, 110–112
  confessional poetry 107
pop culture 54–55, 66
Portmahomack xii
*Portrait of the Artist as a Young Man, A* 63
postmodern literary climate 81
poverty 9
powerlessness 22
privacy 8
prostitution 86, 88–89, 90, 92, 97–98
PTSD (Post-Traumatic Stress Disorder) 35
puberty 48–49
publication
  avoidance of 1, 9, 54
*Publisher's Weekly* 16

135

# INDEX

publishing 3, 7
Pullman, Philip 69

racism 115
rape 60, 97
rejection 12
repetition 19, 29–30, 34, 47, 54, 64–65, 72, 82, 99, 107, 115
resilience 25
revenge 98
ritual 48
romance 1, 86, 107–108

St Giles 84, 88, 90, 92
St James Story Award 12
Saltire Society Book of the Year xiv, 69
Saltire Society First Book of the Year xii, 14
satire 59, 96
school, primary 8
science fiction 53, 61, 69, 71, 79
Scotland 111
   Highlands of xii, 1, 11, 13, 63, 66, 114
   move to 11, 82
   travel through 26, 28
*Scotsman, The* 38, 39, 43, 111
Scottish Arts Council Bursary 12
'Scottish by formation' 14
Scottish Poetry Library 109
setting 13
sex, sexual language 20, 41, 64, 74, 89
*Sex for One: The Joy of Self-Loving* 85
sexuality 8, 28, 63
Shakespeare, William 88, 98
Shelley, Mary 45
short stories 1, 3, 7, 13, 14, 15, 31, 81, 100
short-story database, Faber's personal 11–12
Simpson, Helen (copy editor) 61–64, 84

slavery 100
Smith, Ali 39
Stallone, Sylvester 63
sublime, the 67–68
suicidal fantasies 35–36, 40
Suicide Point 16
*Sunday Herald* 33
*Sunday Times* 85
surgical modification 59–60, 65–66 (see also cosmetic surgery)

Tainto'lilith and Marko'cain 45–51
Tarrel Farm xii
technology 57, 74
   computers 54–55, 74
tenderness 17–18
Tennyson, Alfred 34, 86
terminology
   medium-sized stories 31
   novella 31
testaments (testicles) 49
*Thirty-Nine Steps, The* 34
thrillers 1, 66
Thurber, James 116
time, approaches to writing about 26–29
*Time* magazine 97
*Times, The* 38
*Titus Andronicus* 98
tone 2, 13, 41, 97, 102, 105, 111, 115
Tong, Su 69
tragedy 86
translation xii, 25, 69
transnational fiction 15
transnationalism 1
Transworld xiv
trauma 8, 20, 22, 60, 66, 98, 112
travel 8
*Trick is to Keep Breathing, The* 63
tropes 2, 76, 79, 96, 108

# INDEX

Ugrešić, Dubravka 69
uncanny, the 51
*Under the Skin* (film) xiii
  original film option 61
unemployment 11
University of Dundee Canongate
  Archive 4, 59, 62–63

vegetarianism 59
VICTORIA (website) 84
Victorian literature 81, 86–87, 102
Victorian realists (according to
  Kincaid: Eliot, Hardy, James,
  Meredith, Trollope) 96
Victoriana 84, 87

*Washington Post, The* 116
Welsh, Irvine 69
Western culture 46
Whitbread First Novel Award
  xii
Whitby 46
Whitby Abbey 33, 36
Whitby Literary and
  Philosophical Society 33
Wilson, Keith 33

withdrawal from public life xiii
*Withnail and I* 56
Women's Social and Political
  Union 100
Word Perfect 55
World War II 8
Writers and Their Work series 4
writing as a child 8

*You Left Early* 114
Young, Louisa 114, 117
Youren, Eva
  collaboration with 10, 33, 38,
    40, 60, 72–73, 82, 106, 111
  dedications to 62, 106, 112
  editorial advice from 10
  family of 11
  illness and death of 1, 4, 53,
    68, 105–112 (see also Faber,
    Michel, books, *Undying: A
    Love Story*)
  marriage to xii
  reading preferences 26
  relationship with xi

Zlosnik, Sue 45–46

137

Printed and bound by CPI Group (UK) Ltd, Croydon, CR0 4YY
10/08/2023

03245629-0001